101 Science Activities

by Trudy Aarons, Francine Koelsch

Illustrations by Francine Koelsch

Games, Gameboards and Learning Centers
for Early Childhood Education
and Special Needs Children

**Communication
Skill Builders**
3130 N. Dodge Blvd. / P.O. Box 42050
Tucson, Arizona 85733
(602) 323-7500

Other publications by Trudy Aarons and Francine Koelsch...

101 Reading Activities

101 Math Activities

101 Language Arts Activities

Peel & Put® Reading Program Activity Manual

©1984 by

Communication Skill Builders, Inc.
3130 N. Dodge Blvd./P.O. Box 42050
Tucson, Arizona 85733
(602) 323-7500

All rights reserved. Permission is granted for the user to photocopy and to make duplicating masters of those pages so indicated in limited form for instructional or administrative use only. No other parts of this book may be reproduced or transmitted in any form or by any means, electronic or mechanical, including photocopying and recording, or by any information storage and retrieval system, without written permission from the Publisher.

ISBN-0-88450-879-X   Catalog No. 7018

10 9 8 7 6 5 4 3
Printed in the United States of America

ABOUT THE AUTHORS

Trudy Aarons and **Francine Koelsch** are teachers in the East Hartford, Connecticut, school system. They are co-authors of Make-A-Game Workshop and since 1973 have conducted workshops for parents and educators throughout southern New England. Both authors received the master's degree from Central Connecticut State College.

This is the fourth in a series of "101" activity books authored by Trudy Aarons and Francine Koelsch for Communication Skill Builders.

DUPLICATING

You may prefer to copy the designated reproducible materials by using stencils or spirit masters. It is not necessary to tear pages out of this book. Make a single photocopy of the desired page. Use that photocopy to make a stencil or spirit master on a thermal copier.

CONTENTS

- HOW TO BEGIN 1
- GAMES CONSTRUCTION 1
- EXPLORING PROPERTIES 3
  - THE SENSES
    - Touch
      - Touch and Match 7
      - Name What You Feel 8
    - Sight
      - Match the Logo 9
    - Smell
      - Match the Smell 10
      - The Nose Knows 11
    - Hearing
      - Which Can You Hear? 12
      - Name That Sound 13
    - Taste
      - Mystery Fruit 14
    - The Senses Worksheet 15
  - SHAPES
    - Simple Shapes
      - Shape Family 19
      - Shape Books 20
    - Complex Shapes
      - What's In My Circle? 21
      - Defend Your Choice 22
      - Finding the Answer 23
    - Shapes Worksheet 24
  - SIZES, WEIGHTS, MEASUREMENTS
    - Sizes
      - The Toast Game 27
      - Is It Bigger Than a Dragon? 28
      - Grow or Shrink? 29
    - Weights
      - Sink or Float? 30
      - Get On the Scale 31
      - Weigh It 32
    - Measurements
      - Guesstimation 34
      - Graph It 35
      - Measure Treasure Hunt 36
    - Sizes, Weights, Measurements Worksheet 37
  - COLORS
    - Creating Colors
      - Color Paddles 41
      - Testing—1, 2, 3 42
      - Window Painting 43
      - Mix the Chalk 44
    - Discovering Colors
      - Berry Prints 46
      - The Rainbow 47
      - They Are Always the Same 48
      - Color Wheel 49
      - Only Room for One 50
    - Color Worksheet 51

MAGNETS
Simple Magnets
- The Magnet Test 55
- Pick It Up 56
- Attractive Puppets 57
- Is It Attractive? 58

Complex Magnets
- Make a Magnet 60
- I'm Powerful! 61
- North or South? 62
- The Electromagnet 63

Magnet Worksheet 64

CULMINATING ACTIVITY: Exploring Properties 65

EXPLORING LIVING THINGS 67

PLANTS
Classifying Plants
- What Will I Be? 71
- Match-a-Seed 72

Discovering Plants
- Watch It Grow! 73
- Wake It Up 74
- Change the Color 75
- Upside Down and All Around 76
- We Need the Light 77
- The Growing Experiment 78

Plant Worksheet 79

ANIMALS
Classifying Animals
- Animal Babies 83
- Where Can I Be Found? 84
- The Egg Puzzle 85
- The Foot Path 86

Life Cycles of Animals
- Which Came First? 87

Environments of Animals
- Search for Me 88
- How Are They the Same? 90
- Animal Homes 92

Animals Worksheet 93

CULMINATING ACTIVITY: Exploring Living Things 94

EXPLORING THE ENVIRONMENT 95

SEASONS
Observing the Seasons
- Preserve a Branch 99
- Adopt a Tree 100
- Pumpkin Activities 102
- Leaf Activities 103
- Snow Art 104

Naming the Seasons
- Spin a Season 105
- The Seasons Bulletin Board 106
- Get Me Home 107

Seasons Worksheet 108

WATER
Properties of Water
- Fresh Water/Salt Water 111
- Warm Water/Cold Water 112
- Make It Bigger 113

Water Vapor
- Disappearing Water 114
- Water from Air 115

Pollution
- Exploring Underwater 116
- Clean It Up 117
- Clean Up the Stream 118

Water Worksheet 119

AIR
Properties of Air
- Is It There? 123
- Burn Out 124
- Don't Get Wet 125

Moving Air
- Straw Painting 126
- Add-a-Straw 127
- Fun with Air 128
- North, East, South, or West? 130
- Which Way? 131

Air Worksheet 132

WEATHER
Instruments
- Blow It Up 135
- The Thermometer 136
- A Barometer 137

Weather Terms
- Weather Record 138
- Making Fog 140
- The Weather Watch 141
- Measure the Wind 142
- Find the Mystery Weather Word 143

Weather Worksheet 144

CULMINATING ACTIVITY: Exploring the Environment

HOW TO BEGIN

101 Science Activities incorporates a variety of science experiences that develop creative and critical thinking. The children will discover basic scientific concepts, principles, and theories through experiments, games, creative activities, and problem solving.

101 Science Activities has three units: Exploring Properties, Exploring Living Things, and Exploring the Environment. At the end of each unit there is a culminating activity that can be used as a post-test for each concept.

The concepts presented in the book have been ordered from the simple to the complex. The activities develop important critical thinking processes through observing, classifying, predicting, communicating, inferring, measuring, experimenting, and making assumptions.

GAMES CONSTRUCTION

Beginnings can be the hardest part of a project. To help you begin, we've listed the materials that have worked best for us, and some avoidable pitfalls.

Materials

★ Folding bristol works best for table gameboards and card games. It is flexible, sturdy, and comes in an assortment of colors and sizes.

★ Bristol board is heavier than folding bristol. It is excellent for wall and bulletin board learning stations and for large floor games.

★ Water-based marking pens are colorful and will make your games attractive. Never use any permanent types of marking pens. They have an oil base that will eventually cause the colors to "bleed."

★ Clear adhesive plastic is a must to cover all your games if you wish them to last any length of time.

★ Don't worry if you are not artistic. Pictures for your games can be found in seals and workbooks. *Peel & Put®* pictures available through Communication Skill Builders are excellent.

Avoidable Pitfalls

★ When you make a game with cards, cut the cards apart after you have covered them with plastic.

★ Paper-punch a hole in the end of the pointer when making a spinner from bristol board. Place a paper fastener through the hole and push it through the spinner. Loosen up the fastener and it will spin freely.

★ Make sure the children have all the necessary entry behaviors in order to play the game. Demonstrate how to play the activity before putting out the game.

★ Establish a routine with your class for using the activities. For example: (1) the correct number of players, (2) completing the activity before choosing another, (3) checking with the teacher when the activity is completed, (4) putting away the activity.

★ Storage of the activity is important. Each activity should have a specific place where it belongs and an appropriate container. It should be visible to the children and within their reach. Pieces of the activity should be kept together.

Exploring Properties

The purpose of the Properties unit is to help the children process information about their environment. It gives them the vocabulary necessary to classify, measure, and observe.

The activities in this unit will help to develop the children's awareness of the senses, shapes, sizes, weights, measurements, colors, and magnets.

At the conclusion of the unit the children should be able to use their newly acquired vocabulary to observe, classify, group, describe, compare, and contrast objects.

The Senses

TOUCH AND MATCH

Objective
   To match objects, using the sense of touch

Materials
   Bristol board, 12" x 12"
   Folding bristol
   Marking pen, ruler, scissors, paste or glue
   Pieces of material with distinctive textures
      (terry cloth, velvet, fur, sandpaper, foil, wool, vinyl, sponge, corduroy, etc.)
   An envelope
   A blindfold (optional)

Making the Game
   1. Mark off eight 2" squares on the bristol board, as illustrated.
   2. Cut out eight 2" pieces of material. Paste one piece on each square on the board.
   3. Mark off eight 2" squares on the folding bristol. Cut into cards.
   4. Cut out a duplicate set of pieces of material. Paste one piece on each card.
   5. Place the cards in an envelope.

Playing the Game
   1. The child tactilely examines each square on the board and discusses whether the material feels soft, hard, smooth, bumpy, rough, etc.
   2. With eyes closed (or using the blindfold), the child reaches into the envelope and feels each square.
   3. As each square is identified according to its texture, the child places it next to its match on the board.

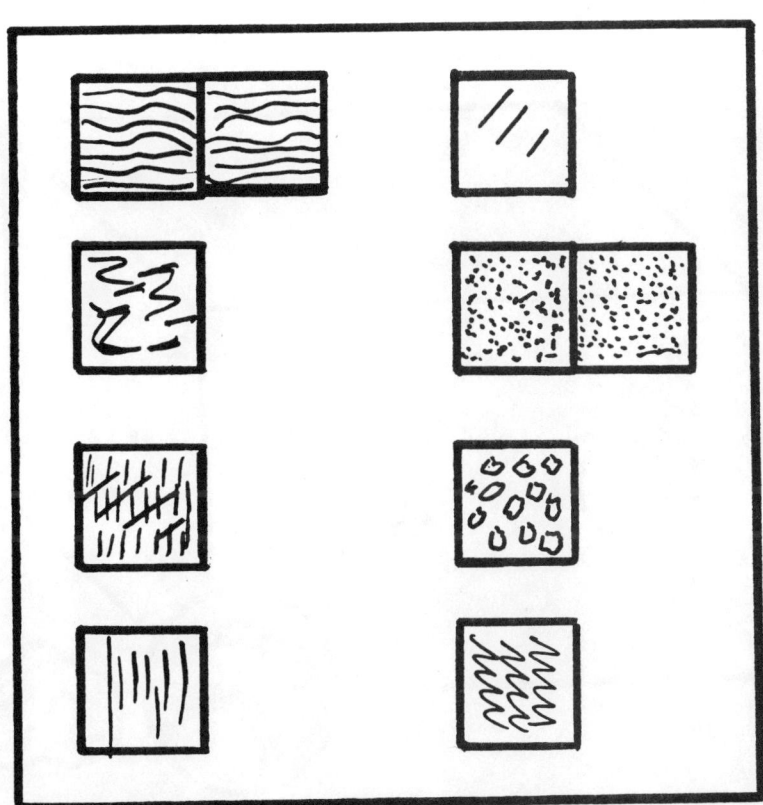

8 ■ *Exploring Properties/The Senses: Touch*

NAME WHAT YOU FEEL

Objective
To identify objects by the sense of touch

Materials
Cardboard box
Scissors or razor knife
A pair of socks
Stapler
Objects with distinctive textures and shapes
(ball, rock, bottle, cotton, ball of yarn, sandpaper)

Making the Game
1. Cut off the top of a cardboard box.
2. Cut two holes in the bottom of the box, as illustrated.
3. Cut off the foot of each sock. Staple a cuff to the inside of each hole.
4. Turn the box so the opening is in the back of the playing area.

Playing the Game
1. Place all objects in the box.
2. The player places both hands through the socks and feels each object.
3. The player names each object as it is identified by touch.

MATCH THE LOGO

Objective
To match variations of a specific logo

Materials
Bristol board, 20" x 24"
Folding bristol
Marking pen, ruler, scissors or paper cutter, paste or glue, paper punch
25 drapery hooks
30 logos (six each, varying in size and color, from a fast food restaurant, a store, a cereal, a detergent, and a soap)
Clear adhesive plastic

Making the Game
1. Rule the bristol board into 4" squares (five columns of six rows).
2. Paste one logo from each category in each space across the top row.
3. Cover the gameboard with clear adhesive plastic.
4. Attach a drapery hook in the top of each remaining space.
5. Rule the folding bristol into 25 sections, each 2½" x 3½". Paste a logo in each section. Cover with clear adhesive plastic and cut apart into cards.
6. Punch a hole in the top of each card.

Playing the Game
A child may play independently by matching the small cards to the correct category, hanging the cards on the drapery hooks.

Variation
Five children may play the game.
1. All cards are placed face down on the playing area.
2. Each child selects a category in the top row.
3. In turn, the children turn over one card. If the card has a logo in that child's category, the child places the card on a drapery hook under the matching logo.
4. The first child to complete a column wins the game.

MATCH THE SMELL

Objective
 To match identical smells

Materials
 Empty film canisters
 Cotton balls
 Various materials that have distinctive odors
  (lemon juice, floral perfume, onion juice, soap, spices, extracts, etc.)
 Tape
 Colored marking pens

Making the Game
 1. Place a cotton ball in each film canister.
 2. Select a material that has a distinct odor. Sprinkle a few drops of the material on the cotton in two canisters. Put the cap on each canister.
 3. Prepare several sets of canisters. Each set should contain a different odor.
 4. On the bottom of each canister, place tape. Color-code the canisters. The two odors that match should have the same color code.

Playing the Game
 1. The child sits in front of the canisters, uncaps one, and smells the contents.
 2. Uncapping the canisters one at a time, the child matches the odor.
 3. The child looks at the bottom of the canisters. If the colors match, the odor match is correct.

THE NOSE KNOWS

Objective
    To match an object with its smell

Materials
    Bristol board, 12" x 18"
    Folding bristol
    Colored marking pens, ruler
    Scratch 'n Sniff labels
    Paper fasteners
    Paper punch, scissors or paper cutter
    Clear adhesive plastic

Making the Game
1. Rule the bristol board into eight 4½" x 6" sections.
2. In each section, draw a picture of an object shown on the Scratch 'n Sniff labels (lemons, grapes, watermelon, chocolate bars, etc.) or affix a Scratch 'n Sniff label. Cover the gameboard with clear adhesive plastic.
3. Under each picture, place a paper fastener.
4. Rule the folding bristol into eight 2" squares. In each square, place a sticker to correspond to the pictures on the gameboard. Cover with clear adhesive plastic and cut apart into cards.
5. Punch a hole at the top of each card.

Playing the Game
1. The child places the cards, sticker face down, on the playing area.
2. The child names the pictures on the gameboard.
3. The child picks up a card without turning it over, scratches the sticker underneath, smells it, and hooks it under the picture that matches the smell. If the sticker pictures match, the child's match is correct.

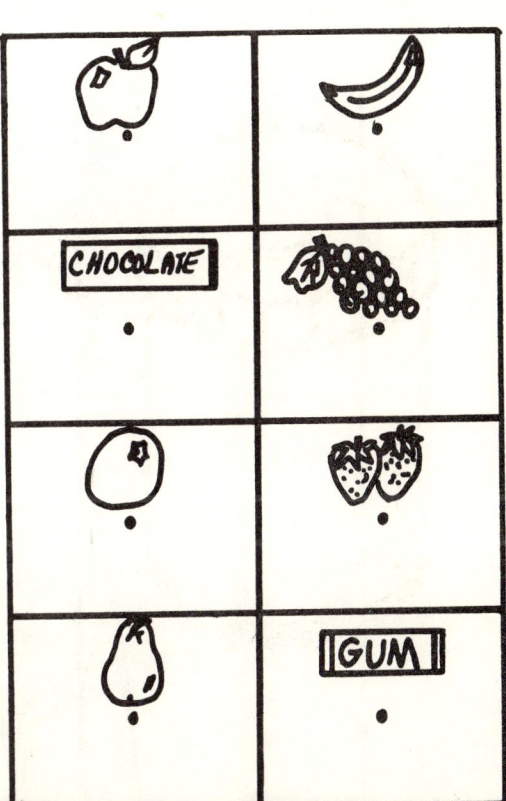

12 ■ *Exploring Properties/The Senses: Hearing*

WHICH CAN YOU HEAR?

Objective
    To identify objects that produce sounds

Materials
    Bristol board, 12" x 18"
    Folding bristol
    Pictures of objects that make a sound
    Pictures of objects that do not make a sound
    Black marking pen, ruler, scissors or paper cutter, paste
    Clear adhesive plastic

Making the Game
1. Divide a piece of bristol board in half by drawing a line with a marking pen. Mark off a 3" border across the top. On one side, draw an ear with a happy face. On the other side, draw an ear with a sad face. Cover the board with clear adhesive plastic.
2. Mark off 4" squares on the folding bristol. On the squares, paste an equal number of pictures of objects that can be heard and objects that do not produce a sound. (Variations may be inside and outside sounds or high and low sounds.)
3. Cover with clear adhesive plastic and cut apart into cards.

Playing the Game
1. All cards are placed face down on the playing area.
2. The child turns over each card, names the picture, discusses whether the object does or doesn't make a sound, and then places the card on the correct side of the board.

NAME THAT SOUND

Objective
> To identify sounds

Materials
> A blindfold
> Scissors, stapler, bell, paper, drum

Making the Game
> Gather the materials necessary to play the game.

Playing the Game
1. The children are seated around a table. The materials are placed in the center of the playing area. The children take turns being blindfolded.
2. The teacher (or a designated child) produces a sound with one of the articles (for example, crushes paper). The blindfolded child guesses the sound, in three tries or less.

To increase difficulty, use objects that require finer discrimination.

14 ■ *Exploring Properties/The Senses: Taste*

MYSTERY FRUIT

Objective
To identify foods by taste

Materials
Margarine containers with opaque lids
Small hole punch (such as a tapestry needle)
Toothpicks
Pieces of fruit (oranges, apples, lemons, pears, bananas, pineapple)
A plate or tray

Making the Game
1. Punch holes in each opaque lid.
2. Place a different fruit in each margarine container.
3. Cover each container with a lid.
4. Place some of each fruit on a plate.

Playing the Game
1. Let the children taste each fruit on the plate and discuss the flavors.
2. Have each child insert a toothpick in a hole in the covered container, spear a piece of fruit, taste the juice on the toothpick, and name the fruit tasted. Each child should have a turn to sample all the fruits.

After each use, the toothpick is discarded and a new one is used. The fruits in the containers should be replenished frequently.

Exploring Properties/The Senses ■ 15

THE SENSES WORKSHEET

Directions to the teacher: Fold along the dotted line; reproduce the worksheet.

Have the children color and cut out the four sets of small pictures (sun, music, ice cream cone, rain).

Discuss music. Ask if you can *see* music, *hear* music, *taste* music, *smell* music, *touch* music. Have the children paste a music picture under the senses that apply.

Repeat the activity for the sun, ice cream cone, and rain.

THE SENSES WORKSHEET

Name _____   Date _____

SEE	HEAR	TASTE	SMELL	TOUCH

© 1984 by Communication Skill Builders, Inc.
This page may be reproduced for instructional use.

Shapes

Exploring Properties/Simple Shapes ■ 19

SHAPE FAMILY

Objective
    To name and identify simple shapes

Materials
    Modeling clay (see recipe below)
    Rolling pin, cookie cutters (optional)

Making the Game

                    Modeling Clay
    2 cups baking soda   1½ cups water
    1 cup cornstarch   Food coloring (optional)

Mix the dry ingredients in a saucepan. Add water. Bring to a boil, stirring constantly. Boil one minute, or to the consistency of moist mashed potatoes. Add food coloring, if desired. Spoon onto a plate and cover with a damp cloth. Cool.

Playing the Game
1. Discuss simple shapes and their properties.
2. Knead the clay. Give each child a piece of clay. Each child makes a "shape person," forming the body from a particular shape and the remaining body parts from smaller pieces of the same shape.
3. Each day, have the children make a different clay person, using the shape discussed that day.
4. Optional: The clay may be rolled out and cut out with cookie cutters.

SHAPE BOOKS

Objective
To name and recognize shapes

Materials
Construction paper, 9" x 12"
Newsprint paper, 9" x 12"
Chart paper
Catalogs and magazines
Stapler
Paste, scissors

Making the Game
1. Make an eight-page booklet by folding four 9" x 12" pieces of newsprint paper in half. Make a cover with colored construction paper. Staple the booklet on the fold.
2. Cut the booklet into a particular shape discussed.

Playing the Game
1. The teacher and the class will make an experience chart of the shapes discussed.
2. The children will make individual "Shape Books" by pasting in catalog and magazine pictures of the particular shapes.

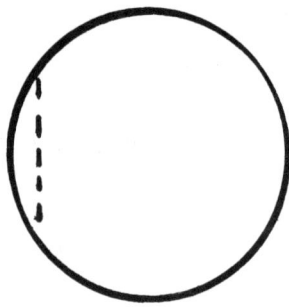

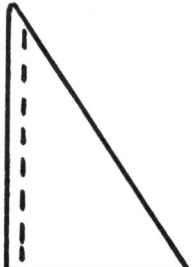

Exploring Properties/Complex Shapes ■ 21

WHAT'S IN MY CIRCLE?

Objective
To sort objects by their shape

Materials
Bristol board
Ruler, marking pen, scissors, paste
Assorted pictures showing objects of various shapes
Yarn, string, or plastic hoops
Clear adhesive plastic

Making the Game
1. Mark off sets of ten 2" square cards on the bristol board. Make one set for each player. Paste on pictures of objects. Each set must have at least one picture representing each shape. Cover with clear adhesive plastic and cut apart into cards.
2. Using bristol board, draw one set of shapes consisting of a circle, triangle, rectangle, cube, sphere, cone, and cylinder. Cover with clear adhesive plastic and cut out the shapes. (The teacher will play with this set of shapes.)

Playing the Game
1. Give one set of cards to each player. Also give each player pieces of yarn, string, or two hoops.
2. Each child sets up two intersecting circles of yarn, as shown in the illustration. In one circle, the child places a set of cards, face up.
3. The teacher places a shape in the other circle.
4. The child determines which picture cards match the shape, and places them in the intersection. (For example, in the illustration, the teacher placed a circle, and the child placed pictures of circular objects—a ball and a wheel—in the area that intersects.)
5. When all the children have taken a turn, they explain why they have made their selections.

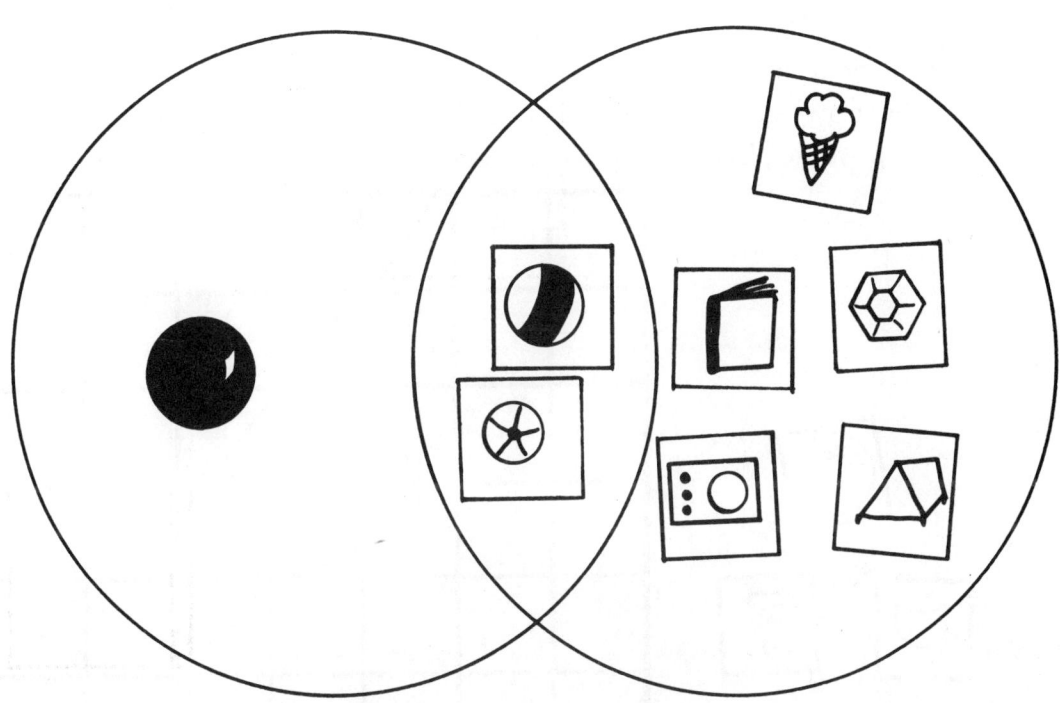

22 ■ *Exploring Properties/Complex Shapes*

DEFEND YOUR CHOICE

Objective
To identify an object according to its shape

Materials
Bristol board, 18" x 21" and a scrap piece
Folding bristol
Marking pen, ruler, scissors
Paper punch, paper fastener
Assorted pictures of objects that clearly illustrate a shape, paste (optional)
Clear adhesive plastic

Making the Game
1. In the center of the bristol board, draw a 6" circle. Divide the rest of the gameboard into 3" squares.
2. Divide the circle into four sections. Mark the sections: WILL ROLL, WILL NOT ROLL, NO FLAT SURFACES, and HAS MORE THAN TWO FLAT SURFACES.
3. Cover the board with clear adhesive plastic.
4. Make a spinner from the scrap piece of bristol board. Cover with plastic, punch a hole at one end, and attach it loosely to the center of the circle with a paper fastener.
5. Rule the folding bristol into 3" squares. In each square, draw a picture of an object that clearly illustrates a shape; or cut out pictures from magazines and paste one on each square. (Simple shapes include a circle, triangle, square, and rectangle; more complex shapes are a cube, cylinder, and cone.)
6. Cover with clear adhesive plastic and cut apart into cards.

Playing the Game
This is a game for two or four players.
1. The cards are evenly divided among the players. They are turned face up on the playing area.
2. The players take turns spinning the spinner and checking their cards to find one that fits the category on the spinner. Cards that fit the category are placed randomly in a space on the board.
3. If another player questions the card, the first player must defend the choice.
4. The first player to place all cards on the board wins the game.

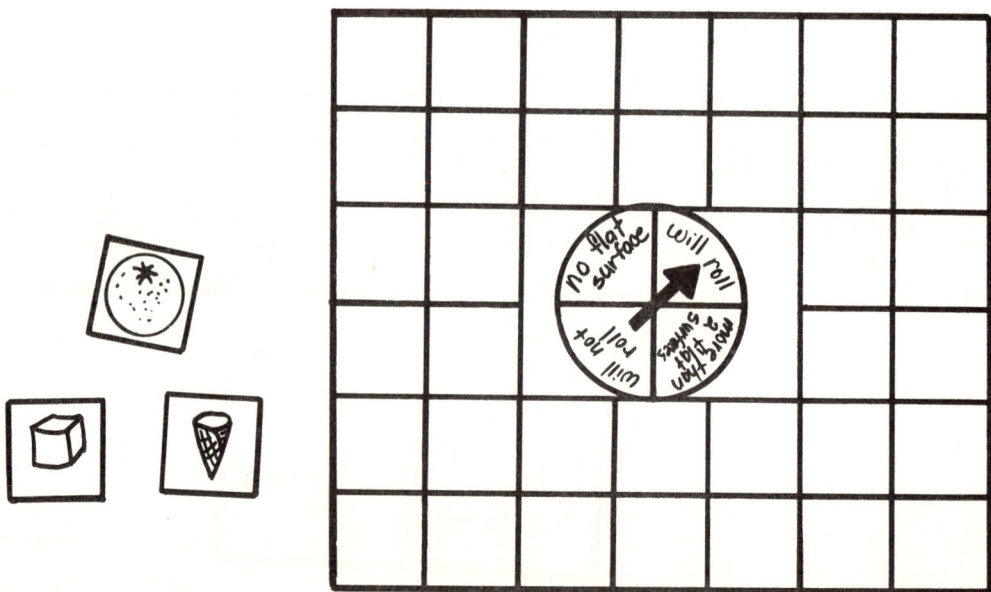

FINDING THE ANSWER

Objective
　　To observe shapes of objects

Materials
　　Bristol board
　　Ruler, marking pen, scissors, paste
　　Small pictures
　　Clear adhesive plastic

Making the Game
1. Rule bristol board into twenty to forty 3" x 6" sections.
2. Divide each section in half. On one side, paste a picture of an object that has a distinct shape. On the other side, write a description (see illustration). The descriptions will depend on the desired degree of difficulty. For example:

Simple Descriptions	More Complex Descriptions
It's a circle	It's a solid
It's a square	It may have all flat surfaces
It's a triangle	It has no corners
It's a rectangle	It rolls
It's round	It will not roll
It's a box	It's spherical

   Designate at least five descriptions of different shapes (four cards of each shape and description).
3. Cover with clear adhesive plastic and cut apart into 3" x 6" cards.

Playing the Game

This game is similar to a domino game.
1. Place one card in the center of the playing area, face up.
2. Distribute the remaining cards equally.
3. The players turn the cards face up in front of them.
4. The players take turns looking at their cards, trying to match either the description on the card in the center with a picture, or the picture on the card in the center with a description. If a match can be made, the player places the matching card in the center so that the picture and description are touching. If a match cannot be made, play continues.
5. The first player to place all cards on the playing area wins the game.

24 ■ Exploring Properties/Shapes

SHAPES WORKSHEET

Directions to the teacher: Fold along the dotted line; reproduce the worksheet.

The children will mark the pictures with more than one symbol. Have them discuss how and why they marked each item.

SHAPES WORKSHEET

Name _____ Date _____

Draw a ◯ around things that roll.
Draw a △ around things that have corners.
Draw a ☐ around things that have one or more flat surfaces.
Draw a ▭ around things that will not roll.

©1984 by Communication Skill Builders, Inc.
This page may be reproduced for instructional use.

Sizes, Weights, Measurements

THE TOAST GAME

Objective
To discriminate sizes

Materials
Assorted pieces of bristol board
Marking pen, ruler, scissors, paste
Pictures of large and small objects
Drapery hooks
Paper punch
Clear adhesive plastic

Making the Game
1. Divide a 12" x 18" piece of bristol board in half.
2. On each side of the board, make a 4" drawing of a piece of toast. Write BIGGER THAN on one side, and SMALLER THAN on the other side. Cover with clear adhesive plastic.
3. In the top center of each piece of toast, place a drapery hook.
4. On bristol board pieces, rule off at least ten sections ranging in size from 1" square to 9" square.
5. Paste pictures of large objects on large sections, and pictures of small objects on small sections. Cover with clear adhesive plastic and cut apart into cards.
6. Punch a hole in the top center of each card.

Playing the Game
1. The child selects squares according to size.
2. In front of the BIGGER THAN side, the child places all the cards that might cover the piece of toast. In front of the SMALLER THAN side, the child places all the cards that might *not* cover the toast.
3. After selections have been made, the child hangs the cards on the drapery hooks one at a time, to self-correct.

For a more difficult task, spread out all the cards and select objects that are in reality bigger than or smaller than the piece of toast, regardless of the size of the square they are pasted on.

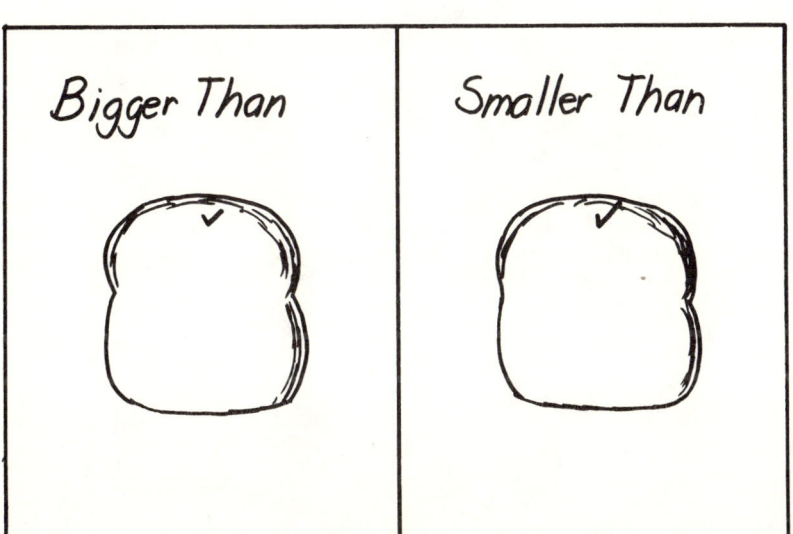

IS IT BIGGER THAN A DRAGON?

Objective
    To compare sizes

Materials
    Bristol board, 12" x 18" and a scrap piece
    Marking pens, ruler
    Paper punch, paper fasteners
    Small pictures, paste (optional)
    Clear adhesive plastic
    Game pieces

Making the Game
1. Draw a dragon in the center of the bristol board. In the middle of the dragon, draw a 5" or 6" circle.
2. Divide the circle into four sections. Mark the sections: LARGER THAN, SMALLER THAN, LOSE A TURN, and TAKE AN EXTRA TURN.
3. Following the illustration, draw or paste pictures to make a gameboard path.
4. Cover the board with clear adhesive plastic.
5. Make a spinner from a scrap piece of bristol board. Cover it with clear plastic, punch a hole at one end, and attach it to the center of the circle with a paper fastener.

Playing the Game
1. Before the game begins, the group selects an object that is to be compared. (Each time the game begins, a new object should be selected.)
2. The players take turns spinning the spinner and moving their game pieces to the closest object that fits the size description. (For example, the comparison object is a car; the player spins LARGER THAN; and moves a game piece to the closest object that is larger than the car.)
3. Play continues until one child reaches the end.

Exploring Properties/Sizes ■ 29

GROW OR SHRINK?

Directions to the teacher: Fold along the dotted line; reproduce the worksheet.

Have the children color and cut out the sets of pictures.

Discuss the pictures. Have the children decide whether each object grows or shrinks. (Answers will vary, depending on the class level.) Have the children paste the pictures in the correct columns.

To extend the activity, reproduce the worksheet without the pictures; and have the children draw pictures of objects they think grow or become smaller.

GROW OR SHRINK

Name _____   Date _____

GROW	SHRINK

© 1984 by Communication Skill Builders, Inc.
This page may be reproduced for instructional use.

30 ■ *Exploring Properties/Weights*

SINK OR FLOAT?

Objective
To observe items that are heavier or lighter than water

Materials
Two plastic containers
Marking pen
A tray
Objects that sink or float
A dishpan
Water

Making the Game
1. On one container, draw a happy face and mark YES. On the other container, draw a sad face and mark NO.
2. Collect the objects that float or sink. Place them all on a tray.
3. Fill a dishpan with water.

Playing the Game
The child selects an object and places it in the water. If the object floats, the child places it in the YES container. If the item sinks, the child places it in the NO container.

GET ON THE SCALE

Objective
To measure objects on a scale

Materials
Objects that weigh less than 16 ounces (two each of the same weight)
Duplicating stencils or copies of worksheets
Postage scale
Pencil

Making the Game
1. Gather objects used for weighing.
2. Prepare worksheets (as shown below) that illustrate the objects you have collected.
3. Duplicate the worksheets.
4. Place the collection of items at the learning center. Set up the postage scale. Put out a worksheet for the day.

Playing the Game
1. The child gathers the items that are estimated to weigh the same as the object of the day.
2. The child weighs all the items selected, and draws a picture of the item that weighs the same as the item of the day.

To extend the activity, tell the children a particular weight for the day. Have them find and draw all the items that weigh that amount.

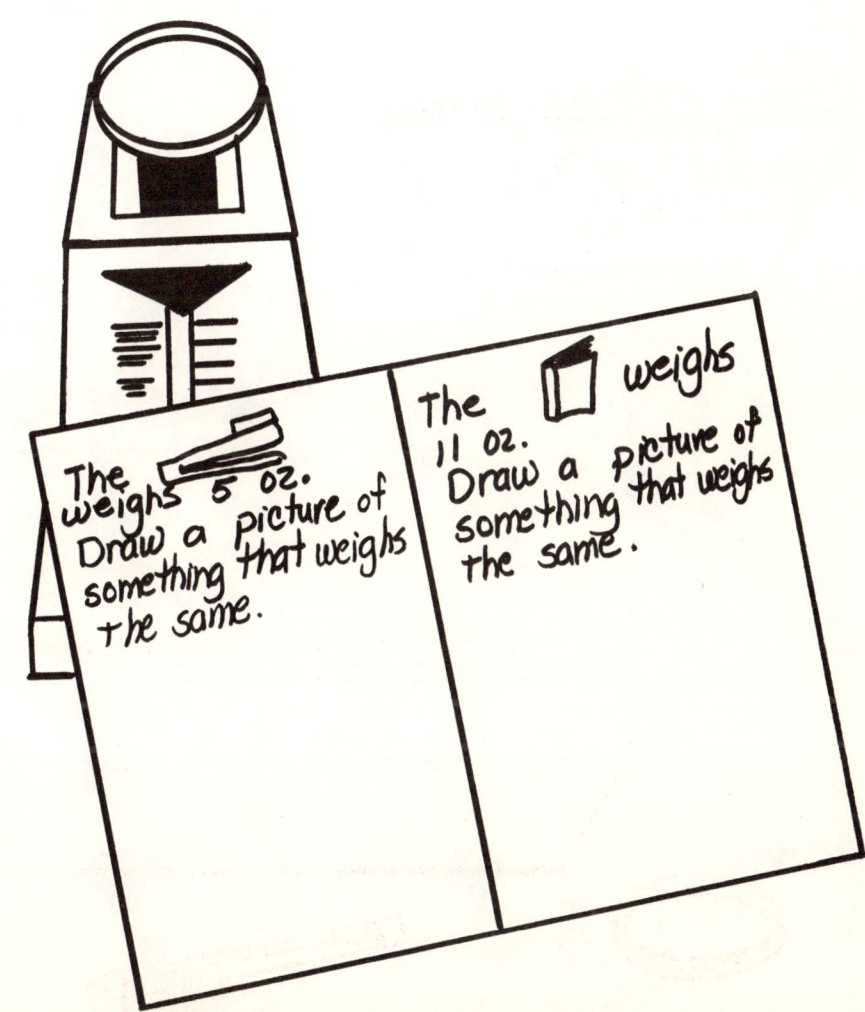

WEIGH IT

Objective
> To compare objects by weight

Materials
> Copies of the worksheet on page 33
>
> Balance scale
>
> Actual objects shown on the worksheet

Making the Game
1. Collect objects for weighing.
2. Reproduce and distribute the worksheet.
3. Set up the scale.

Playing the Game
1. The child selects the objects shown in Box 1 (scissors and ruler), and weighs the two objects to find out which is the heavier.
2. The child circles the picture of the object that is the heavier.
3. The child continues, weighing the objects shown in Box 2 and subsequent boxes and recording the results on the worksheet.

On another day, repeat the exercise but have the child circle the picture of the object that is lighter.

WEIGH IT WORKSHEET

Name _____ Date _____

Weigh the real objects shown in each box. Draw a circle around the object that weighs the most.

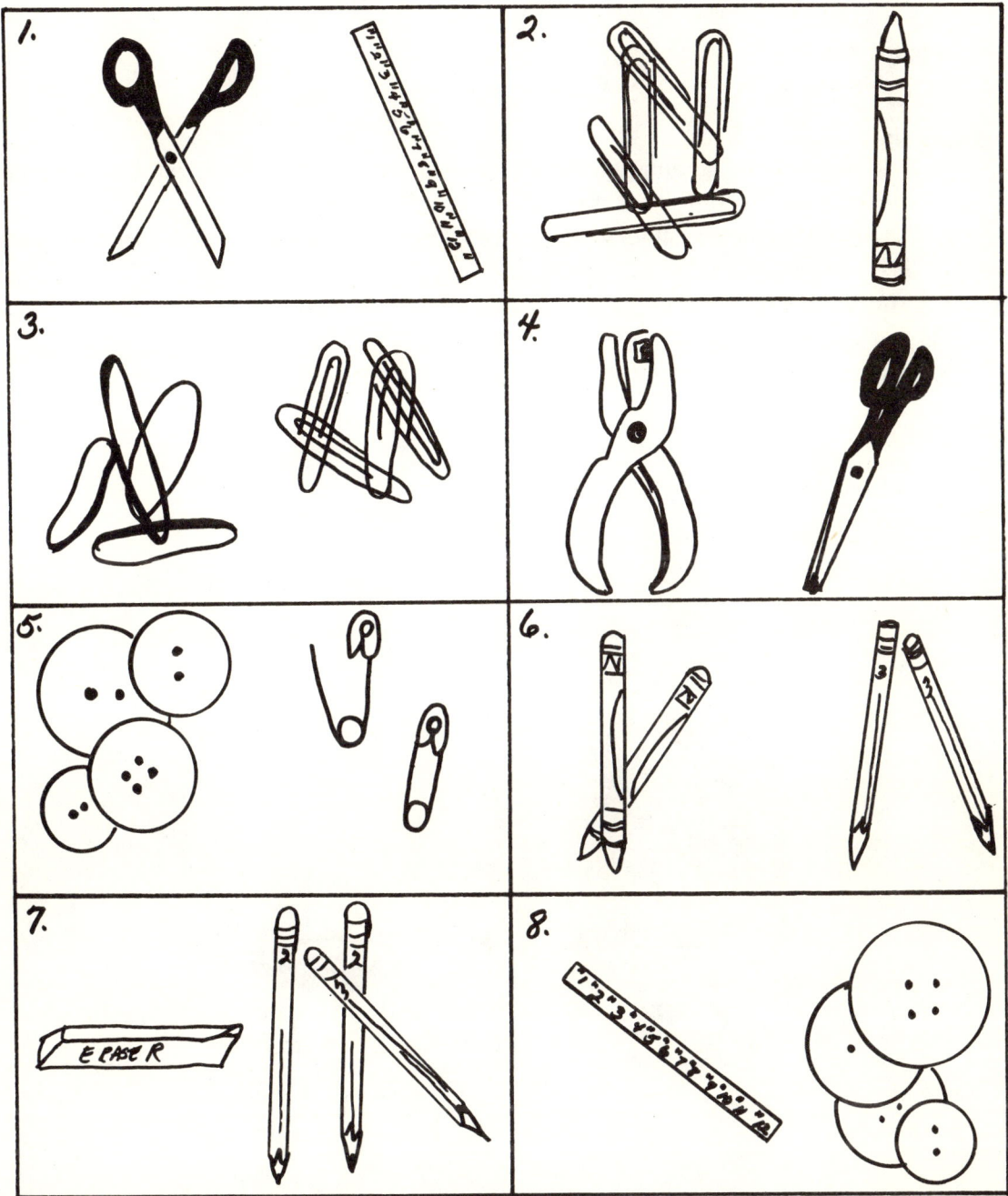

GUESSTIMATION

Objective
To estimate an amount and prove the guesswork

Materials
A dishpan filled with rice (or dried peas or beans)

A measuring cup

Containers of various sizes

Paper

Pencil

Making the Game
Set up the materials at a small table.

Playing the Game
1. The child selects an empty container, estimates how many cups will fill the chosen container, and writes the guess at the top of the paper.
2. The child fills the container with the rice to find the actual number of cups, and writes that number at the bottom of the paper.
3. The child continues the activity with the rest of the containers.

Class discussion should follow.

GRAPH IT

Objective
    To compare sets by using a graph

Materials
    Bristol board, 18" x 24"
    Spring-type clothespins
    Marking pens, ruler, glue
    Labels
    Clear adhesive plastic

Making the Game
1. Decide on a subject to be categorized. Subjects might be:
       Color of eyes
       Number of boys and girls in the classroom
       Ways of getting to school
       Pets
       Colors of clothing worn to school
2. On the labels, write the categories decided upon. Glue the labels onto the clothespins.
3. Rule the bristol board into six 4" columns. Cover the board with clear adhesive plastic.

Playing the Game
1. Place a labeled clothespin at the top of each column.
2. Have each child write or draw in the appropriate column.

Class discussion should follow.

blue eyes	brown eyes	hazel eyes			
Toby Joshua Robert John	Luis Mary	Kendal Susan			

MEASURE TREASURE HUNT

Objective
   To measure length

Materials
   Several objects of varying length
   Ruler or meter stick
   Paper
   Pencil

Making the Game
   Gather the materials.

Playing the Game
  1. Divide the class into small groups.
  2. Write two or three numbers on the board, representing the length of several objects.
  3. The groups race to find the objects with the exact measurements that are written on the board.

  For a more difficult task, select objects with length of ¼- or ½-inch, or centimeters.

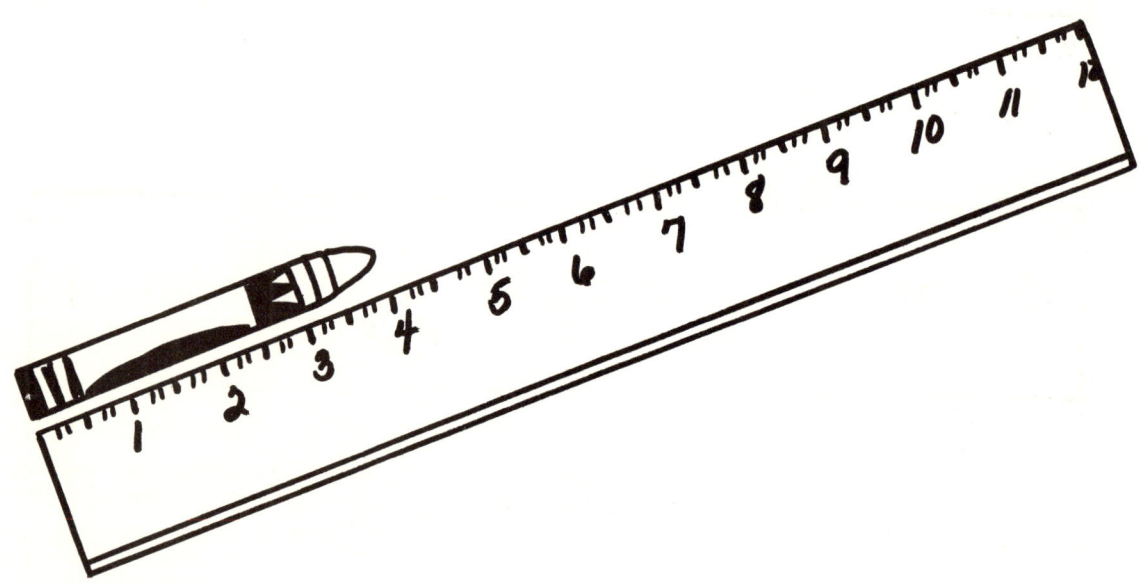

Exploring Properties/Sizes, Weights, Measurements ■ 37

SIZES, WEIGHTS, MEASUREMENTS WORKSHEET

Directions to the teacher: Fold along the dotted line; reproduce the worksheet.

Have the children decide whether to use a scale or a ruler to prove each statement. Then have them cut out and paste the scales and the rulers in the correct spaces.

- -

SIZES, WEIGHTS, MEASUREMENTS WORKSHEET

Name _____   Date _____

1. The crayon is heavier than the pencil.

2. This tree is taller than that tree.

3. My toy car is 7 inches long.

4. The mouse weighs 13 ounces.

5. My hat is 14 inches wide.

6. My cat weighs less than your cat.

©1984 by Communication Skill Builders, Inc.
This page may be reproduced for instructional use.

Colors

Exploring Properties/Creating Colors ■ 41

COLOR PADDLES

Objective
To observe colors

Materials
Bristol board
Ruler, scissors, stapler, glue
Red, blue, and yellow sheets of plastic or cellophane
Tongue depressors

Making the Game
1. Cut the bristol board into six 6" x 4" rectangles. In each rectangle, cut out a 5" x 3" window.
2. Place a sheet of plastic between two window sheets. Staple the corners.
3. Make a handle by gluing a tongue depressor to the bristol board.

Playing the Game
1. Allow the children to explore and observe each color paddle separately.
2. Discuss what happens when two colors are put together.
3. Allow the children to experiment individually.

TESTING—1, 2, 3

Objective
>To observe colors

Materials
>A shoe box
>Clear adhesive plastic
>6 test tubes or plastic tubes
>Red, yellow, and blue food coloring
>Medicine droppers
>Measuring cup
>Water

Making the Game
1. Cover the shoe box with clear adhesive plastic.
2. Turn it over and make six holes equally spaced, large enough to hold the test tubes.

Playing the Game
1. The child puts a test tube in each hole.
2. The child fills the measuring cup with water, and puts some in a test tube.
3. The child puts two drops of a food color into the test tube and shakes it.
4. The child then adds two drops of another color, and observes the new color.

Allow the child to experiment with new combinations.

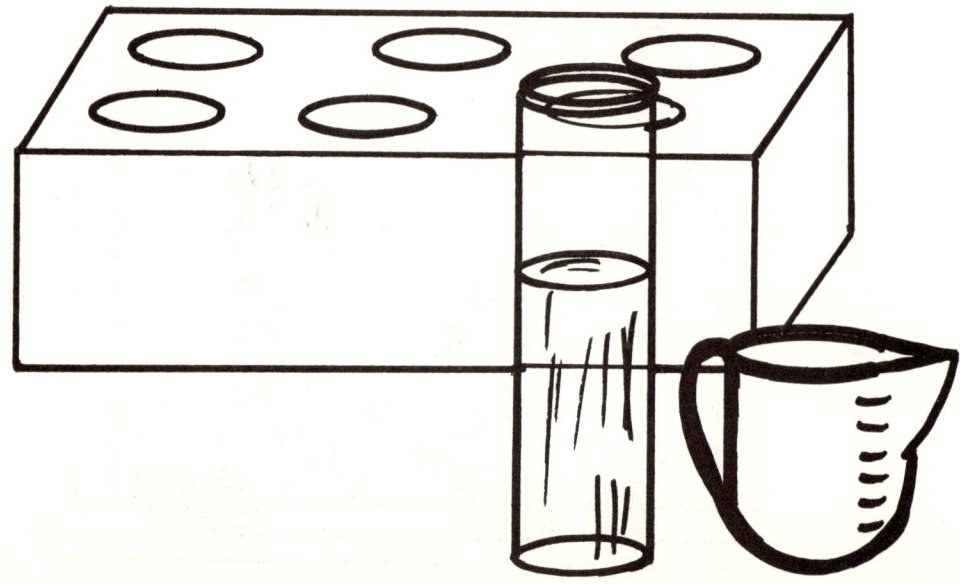

Exploring Properties/Creating Colors ■ 43

WINDOW PAINTING

Objective

To blend primary colors in order to make secondary colors

Materials

Soap flakes
A small bowl
Red, blue, and yellow food coloring
Water
A measuring cup
Nonstick-pan product
Muffin tins
A spoon

Making the Game

Soap Crayons

These amounts make two crayons of one color. To make a primary color, add ½ teaspoon of food coloring. To make a secondary color, add ¼ teaspoon each of two colors.

⅞ cup soap flakes
⅛ cup water
Food coloring

Mix soap flakes and water in a small bowl. Blend until there are no lumps. Add desired food coloring. Spray nonstick-pan product on the muffin tins. Press the mixture into two of the muffin cups. Make a variety of colors, repeating the procedure. Set the muffin tins in a dry place until the soap crayons harden (one or two days).

Playing the Game

Use the soap crayons to draw designs on the windows. When the activity is over, the child can wash the windows clean.

To extend the activity, use soap crayons for body painting for a Halloween or clown unit.

MIX THE CHALK

Objective
To blend primary colors in order to make secondary colors

Materials
Copies of the worksheet on page 45
Red, yellow, and blue chalk

Making the Game
Duplicate the worksheet.

Playing the Game
1. Give each child a worksheet and pieces of red, yellow, and blue chalk.
2. Tell the children to color the pictures as directed, by blending only the appropriate colors.

Exploring Properties/Creating Colors ■ 45

MIX THE CHALK WORKSHEET

Name _____   Date _____

color it orange	color it purple	color it green
color it green	color it orange	color it purple
color it purple	color it green	color it orange

©1984 by Communication Skill Builders, Inc.
This page may be reproduced for instructional use.

BERRY PRINTS

Objective
To observe and use colors in nature

Materials
Ripe berries (blueberries, strawberries, cherries, and raspberries)
Shallow aluminum pans or margarine containers
Coffee filters
A spoon
Paper cups
A knife
A large potato
White paper

Making the Game
1. Crush the berries in the pans or containers. Add a little water.
2. Sieve the berries through the coffee filter into a paper cup.
3. Pour the strained berry juice back into the pans.
4. Cut the potato in half. Draw a design on the face of the potato. Cut away the excess potato around the design.

Playing the Game
Press the potato design into the berry juice and print onto a piece of paper.
Experiment with different berries to observe a variety of colors.

THE RAINBOW

Objective
To discover that a rainbow is made when light shines through water

Materials
A large sheet of white paper

A glass

Water

Making the Game
Set up the equipment.

Playing the Game
1. Place a large piece of white paper on the floor in front of a window.
2. Place a glass full of water on a window ledge in bright sunlight. Extend the glass slightly over the edge of the window sill.
3. Observe and discuss with the class:
    What makes a rainbow?
    What will happen if you take away the light?
    Where is the light shining?
    When have you seen a rainbow?

If it is not a sunny day, shine a strong light through an aquarium filled with water. Attach the white paper to a wall.

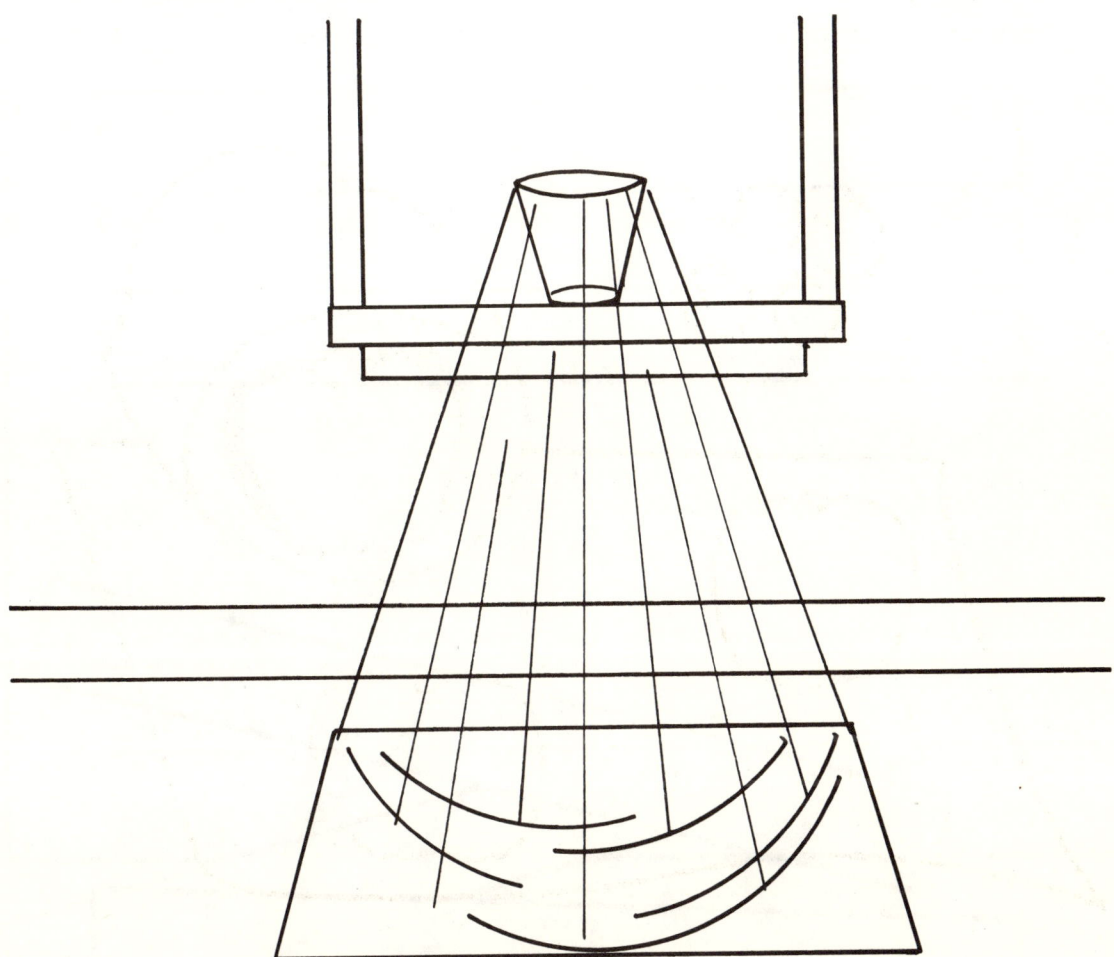

48 ■ *Exploring Properties/Discovering Colors*

THEY ARE ALWAYS THE SAME

Objective
To observe that colors found in a rainbow are always in the same order

Materials
Construction paper in white, violet, blue, green, yellow, orange, and red
Scissors
Paste or glue

Making the Game
Place the materials at the work area.

Playing the Game
1. The child cuts one 2" x 12" strip of each color.
2. The child observes the rainbow made with the water glass or the aquarium (see the Rainbow activity on the preceding page).
3. The child then creates a rainbow by gluing the color strips in the exact order on the white paper.

Discuss whether the colors are always in the same order.

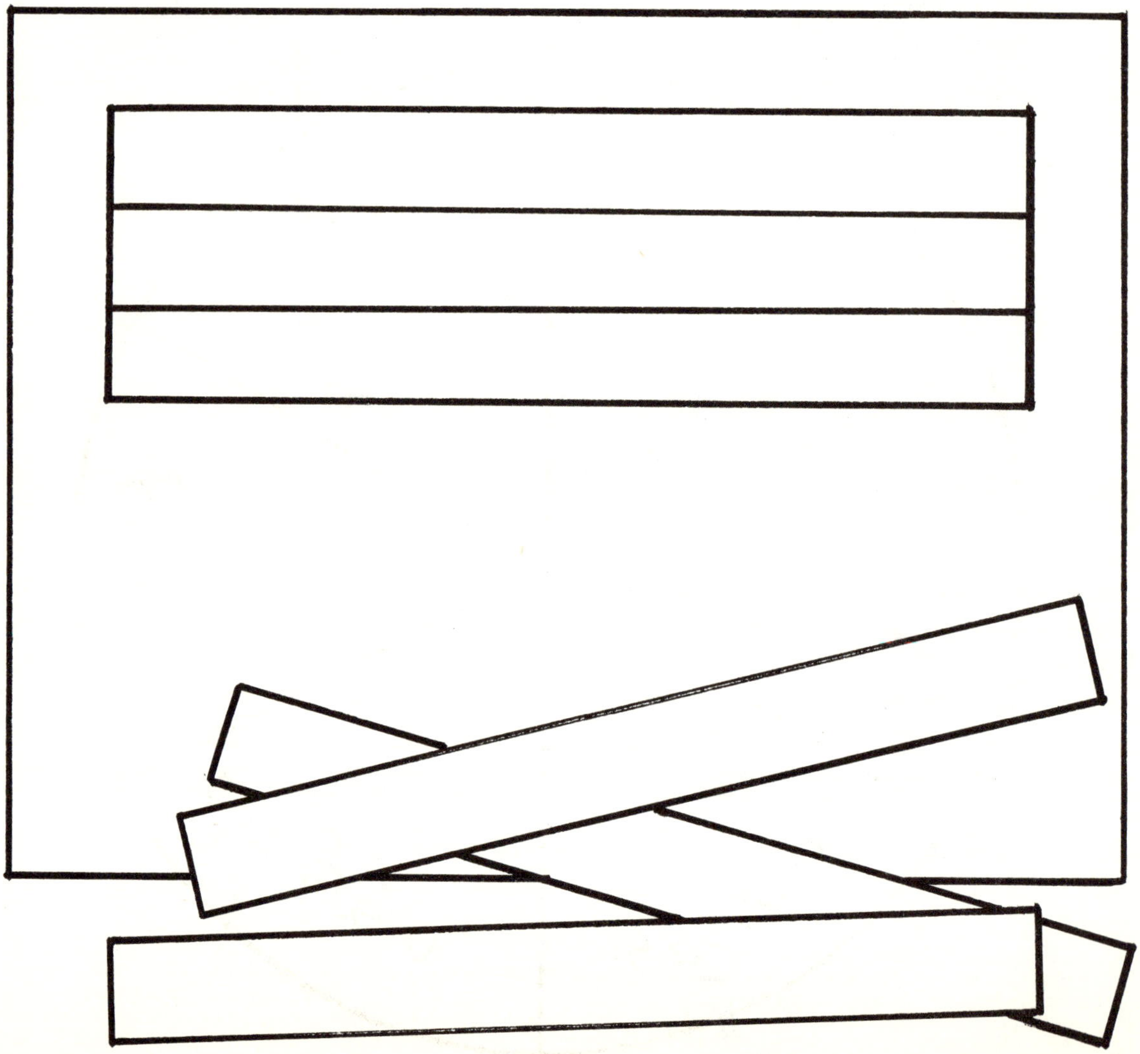

COLOR WHEEL

Objective
To observe that white is the presence of all colors

Materials
White bristol board
Ruler, scissors
Marking pens, water colors, paints, or crayons
A hand drill
Glue
A small nail

Making the Game
1. Cut a 4" circle from bristol board.
2. Divide the circle into six parts. Color the sections red, purple, blue, blue-green, green, and yellow, in that order.
3. Insert a small nail through the center of the circle. Glue it in place.
4. When the glue is dry, set the nail into a hand drill so it turns freely.

Playing the Game
The child will turn the hand drill, experimenting with various speeds. When the correct speed is reached, all colors will blend and the color wheel will appear as a white disc at the end of the drill.

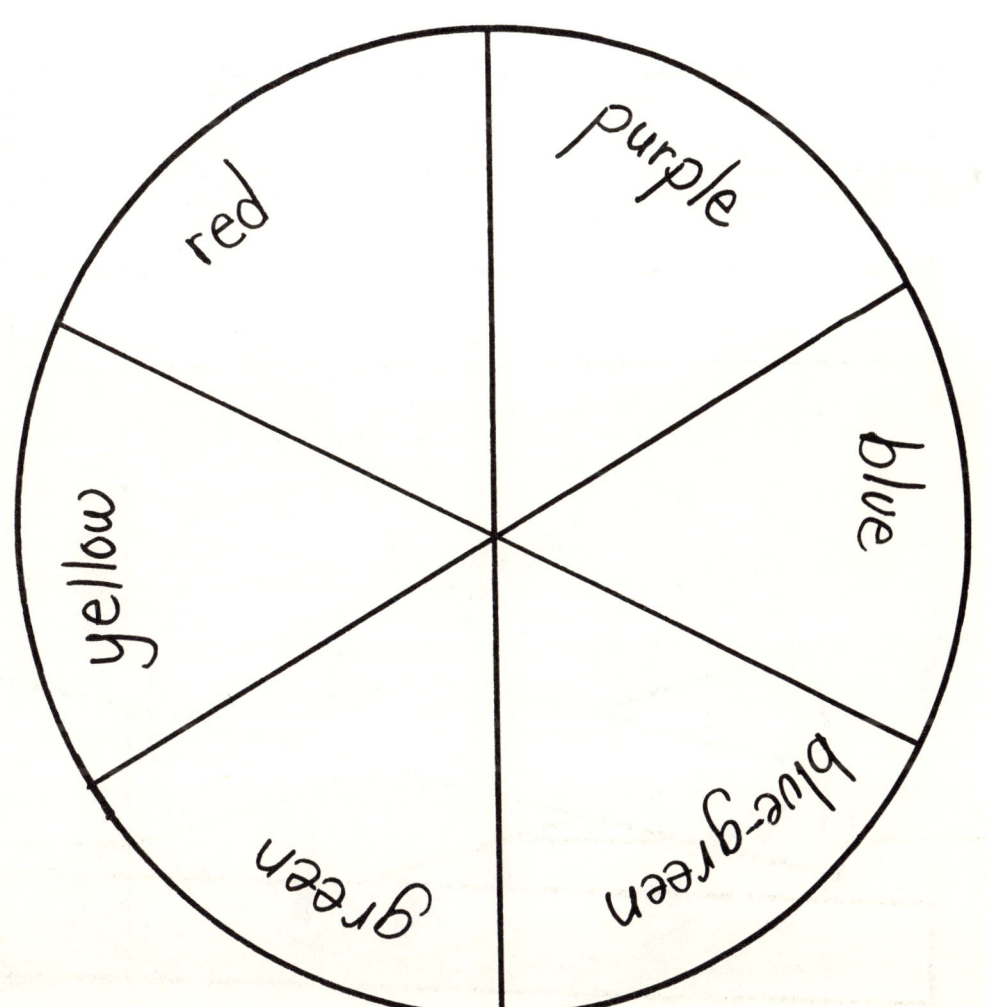

ONLY ROOM FOR ONE

Objective

To observe that there is more than one possible solution to a problem

Materials

White bristol board, 18" x 24"

Blue, green, red, and yellow marking pens

Clear adhesive plastic

44 markers: eleven of each color

Making the Game

1. Draw four intersecting circles, using each colored marking pen once. Each circle will contain seven spaces.
2. Cover the board with clear adhesive plastic.

Playing the Game

1. Divide the markers equally, giving each child a random assortment of colors.
2. The children take turns placing a marker in a space. The marker must be the same color as one of the intersecting lines around that space. Only one marker of each applicable color can be placed in a space. For example, at the intersection of blue, yellow, and red, the space may contain a blue, yellow, or red marker but only one of each color. If there is a marker of the same color in the space, the child must choose either a different space or different color, or forfeit a turn.
3. The child who places all markers first wins the game.

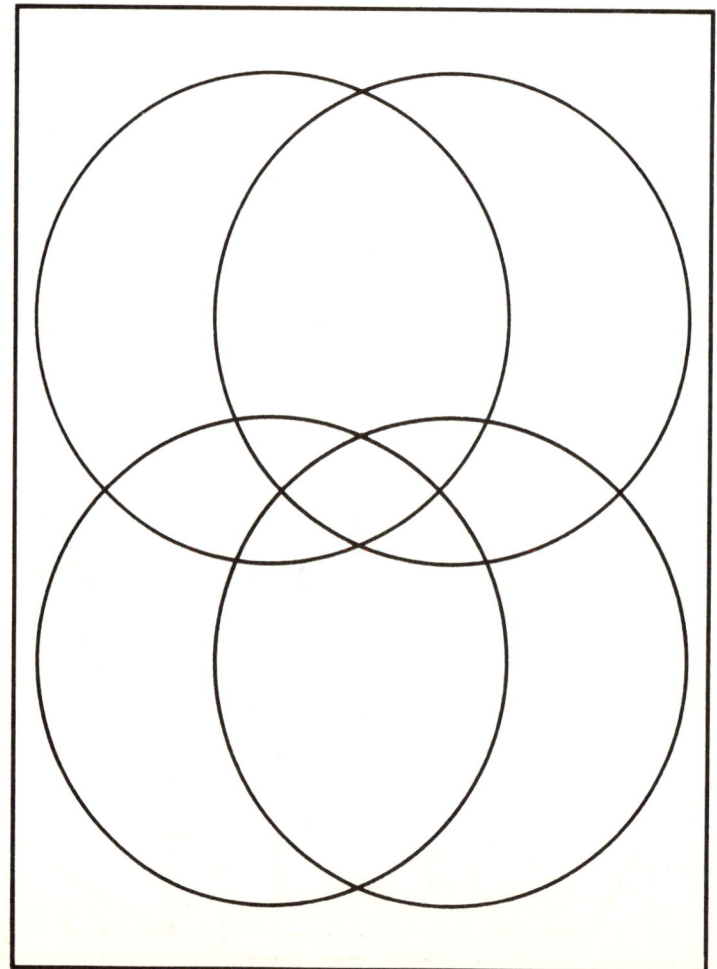

Exploring Properties/Discovering Colors ■ 51

COLOR WORKSHEET

Directions to the teacher: Fold along the dotted line; reproduce the worksheet.

Have the children color and cut as directed. Then discuss where the remaining shapes belong, and why; and which colors are to be used, and why. (Shapes are matched by columns, and colors are matched by rows.) Then have the children paste the cut-out shapes in place and color them.

COLOR WORKSHEET

Name _____ Date _____

1. Color the shapes in Row 1 RED.
   Color the shapes in Row 2 BLUE.
   Color the shapes in Row 3 YELLOW.
   Color the shapes in Row 4 GREEN.

2. Cut out the remaining shapes.

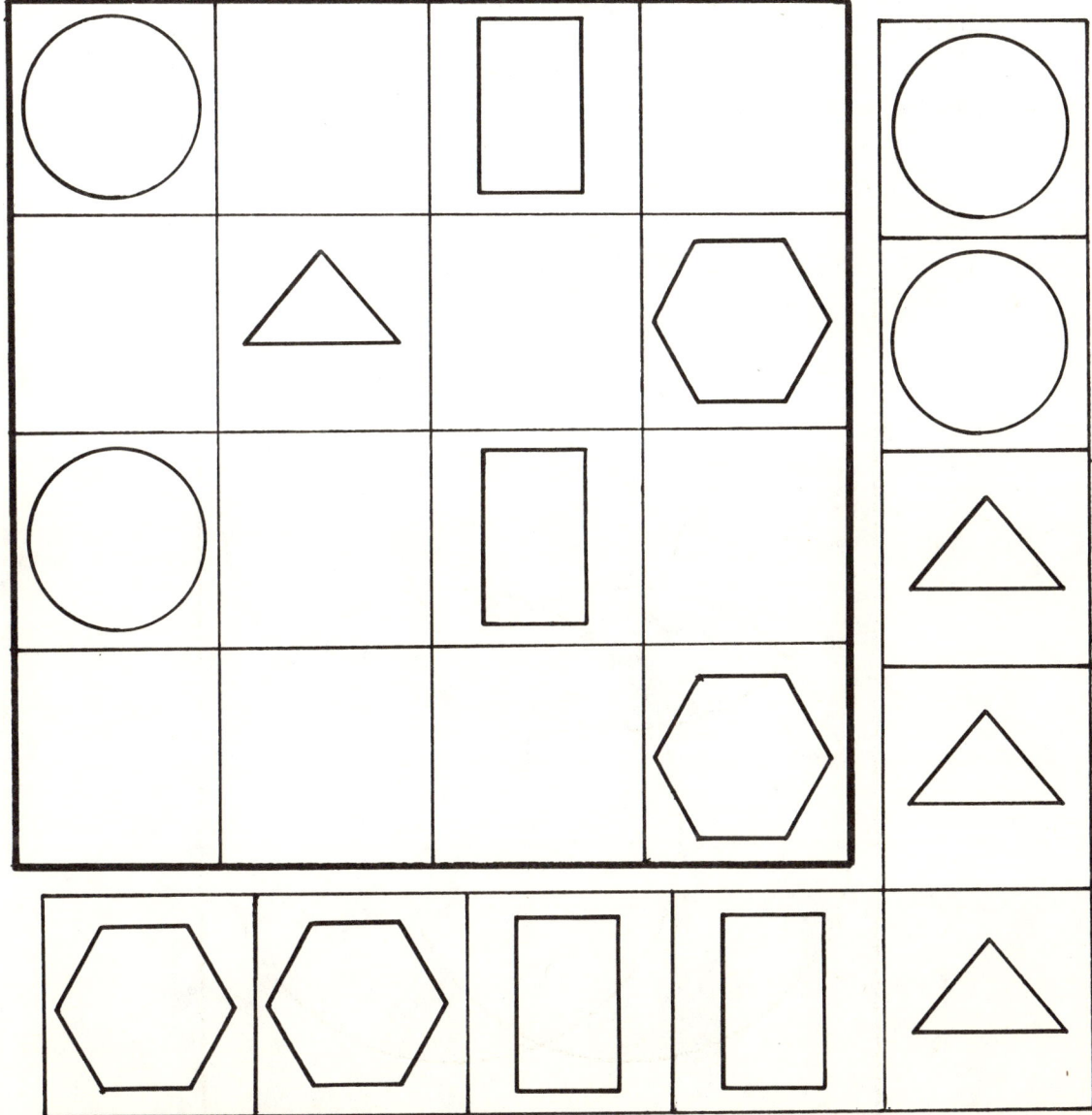

©1984 by Communication Skill Builders, Inc.
This page may be reproduced for instructional use.

Magnets

THE MAGNET TEST

Objective
    To observe that magnets attract certain kinds of objects

Materials
    Two margarine containers
    Marking pens
    Small objects that are magnetic or nonmagnetic
    Magnet
    Tray

Making the Game
1. On one container, draw a happy face and mark YES. On the other container, draw a sad face and mark NO.
2. Place the small objects and the magnet on the tray.

Playing the Game
1. The child tries to pick up each object with the magnet.
2. The child puts the objects that will attract in the YES dish and the objects that will not attract in the NO dish.
3. The child makes observations about the objects that the magnet did attract.

PICK IT UP

Objective
   To observe that magnets are different shapes and sizes

Materials
   A variety of magnets in various sizes (horseshoe, letter u, bar, ring, rod, and disc)
   Bristol board, 18" x 24"
   Ruler, marking pen
   Clear adhesive plastic
   Drapery hooks
   A box of paper clips

Making the Game
1. Rule the bristol board into as many columns as the number of magnets.
2. Trace the shape of a magnet at the top of each column (see illustration).
3. Cover the board with clear adhesive plastic.
4. Place a drapery hook below each picture of a magnet.

Playing the Game
1. The child chooses a magnet and hangs paper clips from the end, one at a time, until the magnet will no longer attract a new clip.
2. The child then makes a chain of the paper clips, and hangs it on the drapery hook under the drawing of the corresponding magnet.
3. The child repeats the procedure for the remaining magnets.
4. The child makes observations about the strength of the magnets by comparing the number of paper clips each magnet holds.

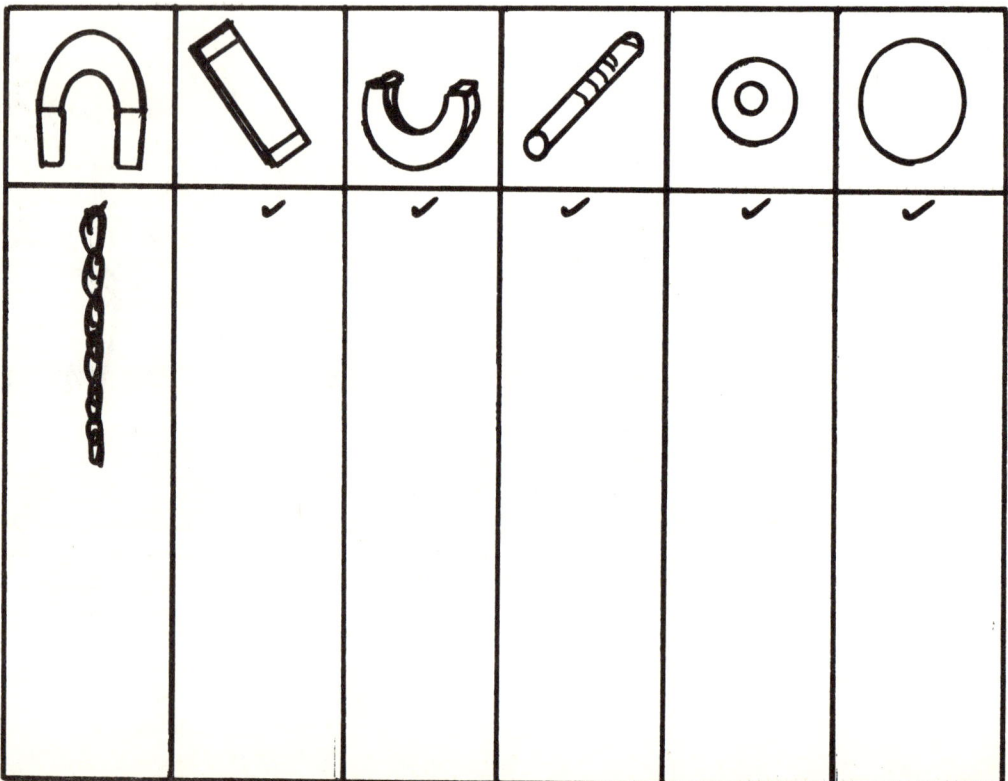

ATTRACTIVE PUPPETS

Objective
To observe that magnets attract through objects

Materials
Bristol board (or a large paper doll on a platform)
Large paper clips
A large cardboard carton
Magnets

Making the Game
1. Draw, color, and cut out a puppet from bristol board.
2. Put a paper clip on the platform at the base of the puppet's feet (see illustration).
3. If desired, decorate the cardboard carton as a puppet stage.

Playing the Game
Turn the cardboard carton on its side. Place the puppet on top of the stage. A child sits inside the carton and manipulates the puppet by moving the magnet under the stage.

IS IT ATTRACTIVE?

Objective

To observe that magnets can attract through some kinds of objects

Materials

Marking pen

A collection of objects, including a glass, a piece of paper, wood, stiff paper, plastic, aluminum foil, cloth, rubber, copper, and zinc

A tray

A magnet

A paper clip

Copies of the worksheet on page 59

Making the Game

1. Draw a copy of the worksheet on page 59 (or make one photocopy of the worksheet for your own use in preparing a stencil, as explained on page iv).
2. In each square, draw a picture of one of the objects.
3. Reproduce the worksheet.
4. Set the collection of objects on the tray.
5. Give each child a magnet, a paper clip, and a worksheet.

Playing the Game

This is an independent activity.

1. The child will experiment with the objects on the tray, placing an object between the magnet and the paper clip.
2. The child will observe those objects through which the magnet will or will not attract the paper clip.
3. The child will check off the appropriate response on the worksheet.

IS IT ATTRACTIVE?

Name _____ Date _____

Did the magnet pick up the paper clip?

	yes 🙂	no 🙁		yes 🙂	no 🙁
	yes 🙂	no 🙁		yes 🙂	no 🙁
	yes 🙂	no 🙁		yes 🙂	no 🙁
	yes 🙂	no 🙁		yes 🙂	no 🙁

©1984 by Communication Skill Builders, Inc.
This page may be reproduced for instructional use.

MAKE A MAGNET

Objective
    To make a magnet from a steel wire

Materials
    A strong magnet
    A paper clip
    Iron filings or bits of steel wool
    A tray
    Wire cutters (optional)

Making the Game
1. Straighten a paper clip.
2. Scatter the iron filings on the tray.

Playing the Game
1. Rub the length of the wire 30 times with the magnet. (Always stroke the wire in the same direction.)
2. Test the wire to see if it picks up the iron filings.

To extend the activity, cut the wire in half, and then cut the halves into smaller pieces. Test the pieces to see if they are still magnetic.

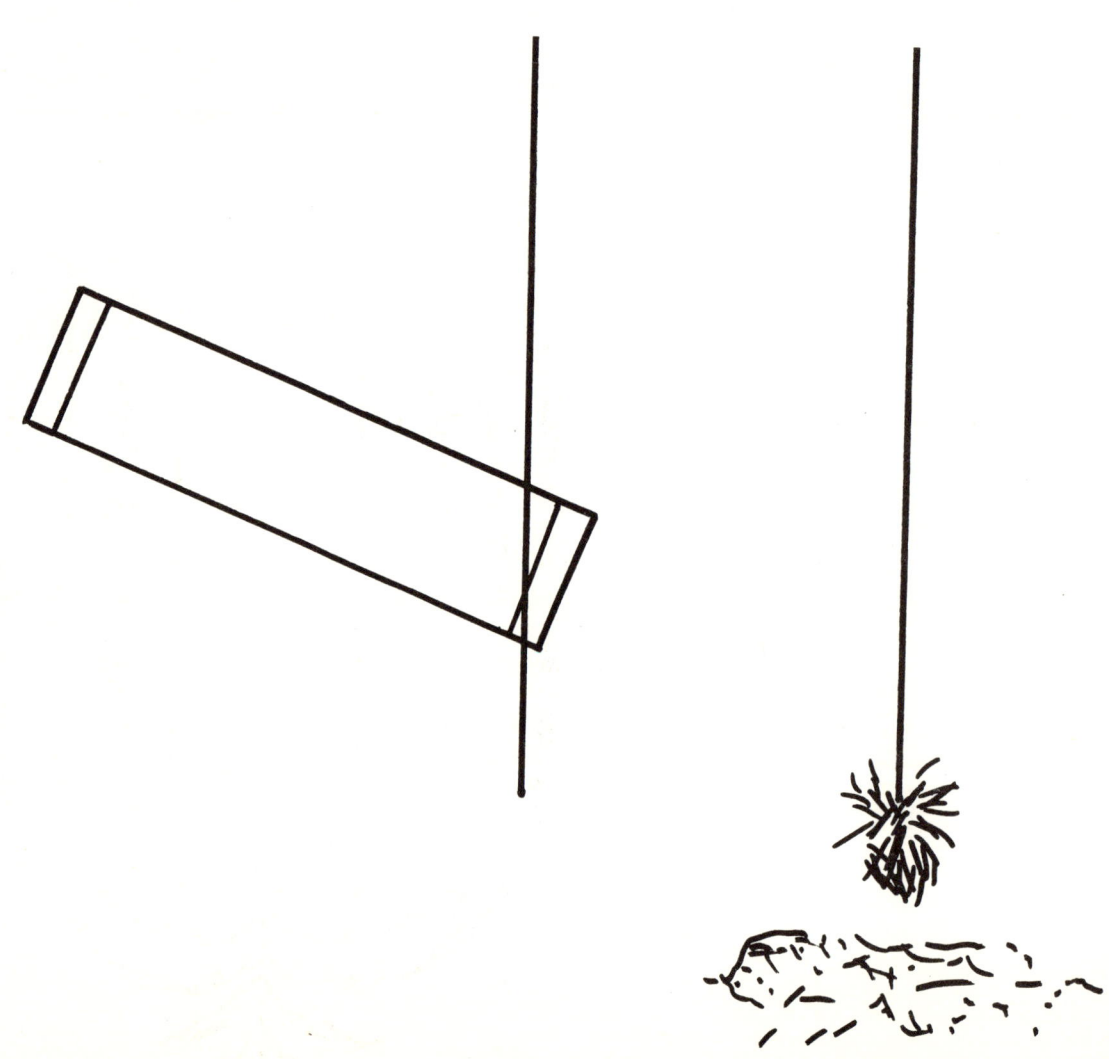

I'M POWERFUL!

Objective
To discover that a magnet has a magnetic field

Materials
A bar magnet
Paper clips
White paper
Iron filings or bits of steel wool

Making the Game
Gather the materials.

Playing the Game
1. Spread the paper clips on the table. Test the magnet by putting it on the table and slowly moving the magnet toward the paper clips. The children should observe the paper clips moving toward the magnet before the magnet touches them. Ask, "Does the magnet have power to pull the paper clips without even touching them?"
2. Sprinkle iron filings evenly over the entire surface of the white paper. Place the bar magnet on the center of the paper. The iron filings will form an elongated circle around the magnet, with most of the filings being at the pole. Ask the children, "What happened to the iron filings?" Discuss why it happened.

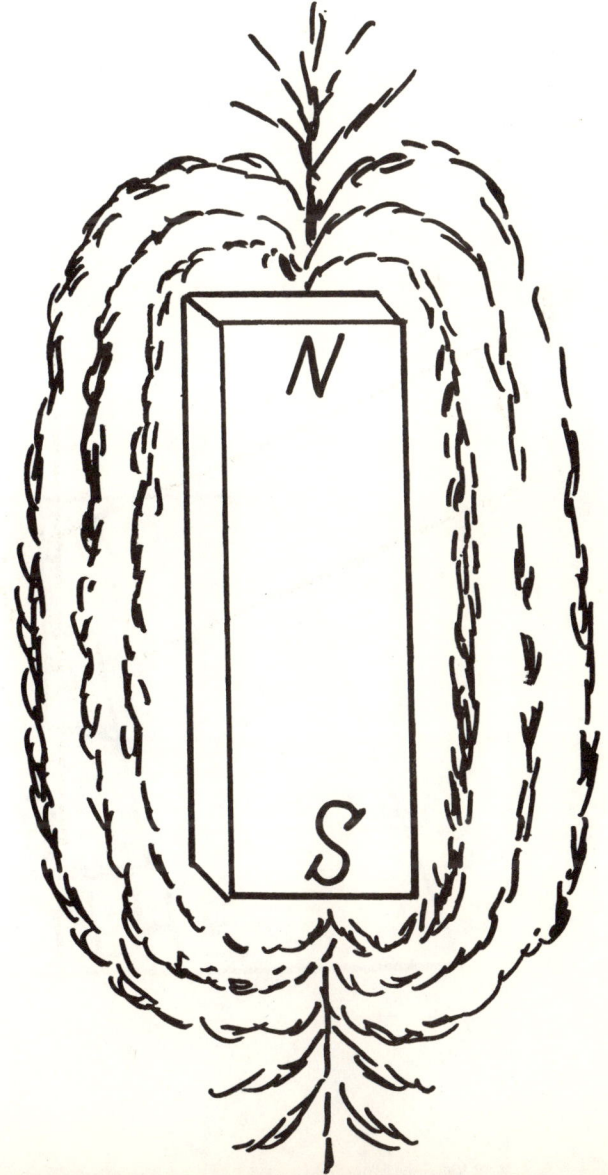

NORTH OR SOUTH?

Objective
To observe that a magnet has a north and south pole

Materials
Paper
A marking pen
A strong bar magnet
A piece of string
Another bar magnet (optional)

Making the Game
1. Mark NORTH on one side of the paper and SOUTH on the other side.
2. Tie a string around the middle of the bar magnet.

Playing the Game
1. Place the paper marked NORTH and SOUTH in the correct direction and away from metal objects.
2. The child suspends the magnet from the string over the paper.
3. When the magnet stops moving, the child observes that the north pole of the magnet is pointing to the north, and the south pole is pointing to the south.

To extend the activity, suspend the bar magnet so that it hangs freely. The children take turns experimenting with a second bar magnet to discover which poles pull or which poles push the suspended magnet. (Like poles will repel, opposite poles will attract.)

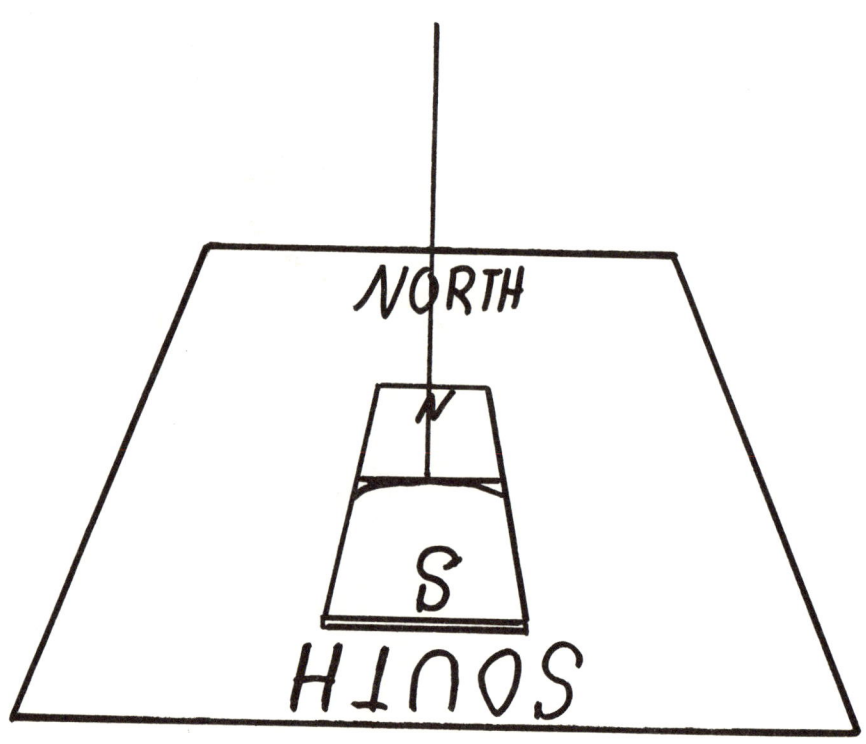

THE ELECTROMAGNET

Objective
To make an electromagnet

Materials
2 feet of insulated wire
A large iron nail
A 6-volt dry cell battery
A collection of objects that will be attracted to a magnet
A tray

Making the Game
1. Wrap the wire around the nail 30 times.
2. Attach each end of the wire to a terminal of the battery.
3. Set up the objects on the tray.

Playing the Game
Before performing this experiment, the teacher may wish to demonstrate that electricity comes from a battery and travels through the wires.

Allow the child to explore the magnetic quality of the nail with the objects on the tray. The child will observe that electricity from the battery passes through the nail and makes it a magnet. The nail is a magnet only when the wires are attached to the battery.

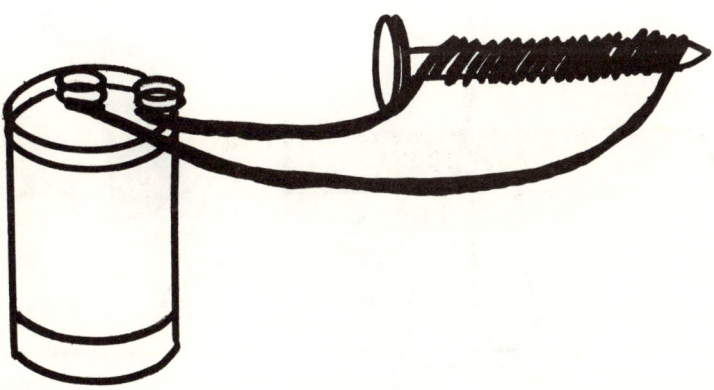

64 ■ *Exploring Properties/Magnets*

MAGNET WORKSHEET

Directions to the teacher: Fold along the dotted line; reproduce the worksheet.

Have the children cut out the happy and sad faces. Tell them to decide whether the object you name is magnetic. Then name the pictures aloud. The children will paste the appropriate happy or sad face in the square by the picture.

....

MAGNET WORKSHEET

Name _____   Date _____

©1984 by Communication Skill Builders, Inc.
This page may be reproduced for instructional use.

EXPLORING PROPERTIES

Objective
To measure the child's understanding of the Properties unit

Materials
A variety of small items or pictures of single items (optional)
Copies of the worksheet on page 66
Scissors, paste, pencils

Making the Game
1. Reproduce the worksheet on page 66.
2. Give each child a worksheet, scissors, paste, and a pencil.
3. Display the collection of items or pictures; or write a list of objects (apple, tree, rain, car, etc.) on the blackboard.

Playing the Game
1. Each child cuts out any nine of the attributes from the worksheet, and pastes them randomly on the tic-tac-toe form.
2. Name an object displayed (or listed on the blackboard). A child who has an attribute that describes the object draws an X through that square on the tic-tac-toe form. (For example, among nine choices the child has selected TASTE, RED, ROUND. You name APPLE. The child crosses out those three attributes that apply to an apple.)
3. The first child to cross off three in a row or diagonally wins the game.

The activity may be played many times by varying the attributes, the objects, or both. For a more difficult task, give harder clues.

EXPLORING PROPERTIES

Name _____   Date _____

see	touch	smell	taste	hear	red	blue
large	small	 ○	 △	white	green	yellow
metal	non-metallic	□	▯	black	orange	brown

Exploring Living Things

This unit provides a basis for introducing the science of biology. It makes the children aware that plants are living things that grow and change. Animals also are living things that grow and change.

The activities in this section will give the child information and firsthand experiences in learning about living things in their environment.

Plants

Exploring Living Things/Classifying Plants ■ 71

WHAT WILL I BE?

Objective
    To match seeds and plants

Materials
    A variety of seeds (corn, pumpkin, orange, apple, lima bean, watermelon, acorn, pea, peach)
    Bristol board
    Ruler, marking pen, glue, scissors
    Clear adhesive plastic

Making the Game
1. Rule the bristol board into 3" x 9" rectangles. In the top half of each rectangle, draw a picture of a plant. On the bottom half, glue the matching seed. Label the seeds, if desired.
2. Cover with clear adhesive plastic.
3. Cut through the center of each rectangle with a puzzle cut.

Playing the Game
    The player puts two puzzle pieces together. If the choice is correct, the pieces will fit.

72 ■ Exploring Living Things/Classifying Plants

MATCH-A-SEED

Objective
To name and match seeds

Materials
A small box
A variety of seeds
(corn, pumpkin, orange, apple, lima bean, watermelon, acorn, pea, peach)
Bristol board, 12" x 18"
Ruler, marking pen
Clear adhesive plastic
Egg carton

Making the Game
1. Label the box SEEDS. Collect and place the seeds in the box.
2. Rule the bristol board into sections. Glue a seed in each section. Label each seed (see the illustration).
3. Cover the board with clear adhesive plastic.

Playing the Game
1. The child takes the seeds from the box and sorts them into the egg carton.
2. The child matches the sorted seeds to the naming board.

Exploring Living Things/Discovering Plants ■ 73

WATCH IT GROW!

Objective
To discover how plants grow

Materials
A jar or glass of water
Toothpicks
A sweet potato

Making the Game
Gather the materials.

Playing the Game
1. Push four or more toothpicks into the potato, just above the center.
2. Submerge the bottom half of the potato by resting the toothpicks on the rim of the glass.
3. Set the glass on a window sill.

It will take two or more weeks for the roots of the plant to grow.

Questions for Discussion
1. What do you see coming out of the potato under the water?
2. What do you see coming out of the part not in the water?
3. How did a new plant grow?

WAKE IT UP

Objective
To observe forcing a branch to bloom

Materials
A small branch (such as forsythia), before the flowers bloom
A jar or glass of water

Making the Game
Gather the materials.

Playing the Game
Place the branch in a jar of water where the children can observe it daily. In a few days, the branch will flower because of the warmth of the room. However, the buds will die and the leaves will never grow because all the stored food in the branch was used.

Questions for Discussion
1. Why did the branch flower when we brought it inside?
2. Why did the buds die?

CHANGE THE COLOR

Objective
   To observe how a plant takes in water

Materials
   A celery stalk with leaves
   Two drinking glasses
   Water
   Food dye

Making the Game
   Collect the materials.

Playing the Game
1. Cut approximately three inches off the bottom of the stalk of celery. Split the center of the celery stalk but don't cut it apart.
2. Fill two glasses with water. In one glass, add enough food dye to make a brightly colored mixture.
3. Place the glasses side by side. Put one celery stalk end into each glass.
4. Allow the celery to remain in the glass overnight. Observe how the dye has traveled up the celery stalk.

Questions for Discussion
1. What happens to the colored water in the celery?
2. Did the colored water travel to all parts of the celery?
3. What do people use to suck up water? (A straw.)

UPSIDE DOWN AND ALL AROUND

Objective
To observe that roots grow downward and plants grow upward

Materials
Lima bean seeds
A jar with straight sides
Paper towels or a blotter
Water

Making the Game
1. Collect the materials.
2. Soak the lima bean seeds overnight in water.

Playing the Game
1. Line the jar with damp paper towels or a blotter.
2. Fill the bottom of the jar with one inch of water.
3. Place the beans in all positions between the side of the jar and the paper towel or blotter. The beans should stick to the sides of the jar.
4. Keep the seeds damp but not wet. In about three days, the seeds will sprout and the class can observe the plants.

Questions for Discussion
1. What came out of the bean seeds?
2. Which are the roots?
3. Which are the plants?
4. Are the seeds pointing in the same direction?
5. In which direction did the roots grow?
6. In which direction did the plants grow?

WE NEED THE LIGHT

Objective
To observe that green plants need sunlight, and that they grow toward the sun

Materials
A green plant
A large box
Scissors

Making the Game
Cut a hole in the side of a large box at the same level as the top of the plant (see the illustration).

Playing the Game
1. Place the plant in the box on a window sill. After several days, the leaves and stems will grow toward the hole.
2. Turn the plant so the leaves point away from the hole. After several days, the plant will turn again toward the light.

Questions for Discussion
1. What happened to the plant?
2. Why does it change growing direction?

78 ■ *Exploring Living Things/Discovering Plants*

THE GROWING EXPERIMENT

Objective
To observe what plants need in order to grow

Materials
Four margarine containers
A marking pen
Potting soil
Marigold or bean seeds
A paper bag
White folding bristol

Making the Game
Collect the materials.

Playing the Game
1. Discuss with the class what plants need in order to grow (sun, soil, water).
2. Number the containers 1, 2, 3, 4.
3. Leave Container 1 empty. Fill Containers 2, 3, and 4 with soil.
4. Place some seeds in all four containers.
5. Place all four containers on a window sill.
6. Cover Container 2 with a paper bag.
7. Every day, water Containers, 1, 2, and 4. Do not water Container 3.
8. Have the children chart the results (see the illustration).

Questions for Discussion
1. Which plant grew the best? Why?
2. What happened to the plant in Container 1? Container 2? Container 3?

Exploring Living Things/Plants ■ 79

PLANT WORKSHEET

Directions to the teacher: Fold along the dotted line; reproduce the worksheet.

Have the children cut out the pictures and paste them in columns, matching the food we eat to the part of the plant it comes from.

Answers: ROOTS: potato, carrots, beets
STEMS: asparagus, rhubarb, celery
LEAVES: cabbage, spinach, lettuce
SEEDS: corn, peas, beans

....

PLANT WORKSHEET

Name _____ Date _____

ROOTS	STEMS	LEAVES	SEEDS
corn	cabbage	carrots	rhubarb
spinach	peas	beets	beans
potato	celery	asparagus	lettuce

©1984 by Communication Skill Builders, Inc.
This page may be reproduced for instructional use.

Animals

Exploring Living Things/Classifying Animals ■ 83

ANIMAL BABIES

Objective
    To match animal mothers to their babies

Materials
    Bristol board, two 9" x 12" pieces
    Folding bristol
    Pictures of mother and animal babies
        (at least 12 different animals, and duplicates of each baby)
    Ruler, marking pen, scissors, glue
    Clear adhesive plastic

Making the Game
1. Rule the bristol boards into three rows and three columns. Cover each gameboard with clear adhesive plastic.
2. Rule the folding bristol into 3" x 4" sections. On each section glue a picture of a mother or a baby animal. Cover with clear adhesive plastic and cut apart into cards.

Playing the Game
This game is for two players. Each player has a gameboard.
1. Separate the Mother and the Baby cards. Place the Mother cards face down in the middle of the playing area.
2. Each player chooses nine different Baby cards. The players place them on their boards, one in each space.
3. The first player turns a Mother card face up. A player who has a matching Baby card on the board turns it face down.
4. The other player takes a turn.
5. The first player to turn over three Baby cards in a row (horizontally, vertically, or diagonally) wins the game.

84 ■ Exploring Living Things/Classifying Animals

WHERE CAN I BE FOUND?

Objective
To classify animals

Materials
Bristol board, 12" x 18"
Folding bristol
Ruler, marking pen, glue
Pictures of farm, zoo, and circus animals
Clear adhesive plastic

Making the Game
1. Following the illustration, draw 2" x 10" rectangles on each side of the bristol board. Divide each rectangle into five 2" spaces.
2. In each space, randomly draw a barn symbol, a zoo symbol, and a circus symbol.
3. Decorate the board and cover it with clear adhesive plastic.
4. Rule the folding bristol into a number of 2" squares.
5. On eight squares, write:
   TAKE 2 CARDS
   TAKE 1 CARD OFF
   SKIP A TURN
   TAKE ANOTHER TURN
6. Glue an animal picture on each remaining section.
7. Cover with clear adhesive plastic and cut apart into cards.

Playing the Game
1. Place the cards face down in the center of the board. Each player chooses a side of the board.
2. In turn, the players take one card and place it on their side of the board, either matching the animal to its home or following the direction on the card.
3. Play continues until a player has filled a row.

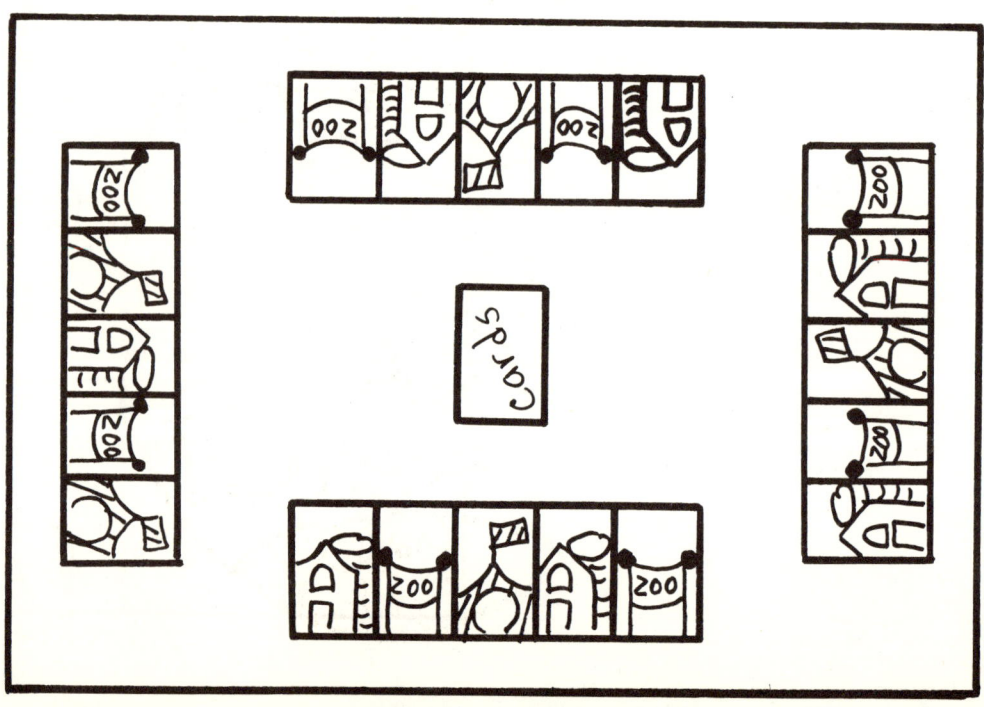

THE EGG PUZZLE

Objective
To name and identify animals hatched from eggs

Materials
Bristol board

12 or more pictures of animals that are hatched from eggs
(ducks, birds, geese, turtles, snakes, alligators)

4 or 6 pictures of animals that are born alive
(whales, dogs, cats, elephants, cows, sheep, horses)

Scissors, glue

Clear adhesive plastic

An envelope

Making the Game
1. Draw an egg (approximately 12" x 18") on a piece of bristol board.
2. On the egg, randomly paste pictures of animals that are hatched from an egg.
3. On another piece of bristol board, paste pictures of animals that are born alive.
4. Cover the boards with clear adhesive plastic.
5. Cut the egg into puzzle pieces, with one picture on each piece. Cut apart the pictures of animals born alive in nonmatching pieces.
6. Place all the pieces into an envelope.

Playing the Game
The child puts the puzzle pieces together to form the egg, finding that only the pieces showing animals hatched from eggs will fit together to make the egg.

86 ■ *Exploring Living Things/Classifying Animals*

THE FOOT PATH

Objective

To observe important animal characteristics

Materials

Bristol board, 12" x 18"

Folding bristol

Marking pens, ruler, scissors, glue

Pictures of animals that have paws, claws, or hooves

Clear adhesive plastic

Game pieces

Making the Game

1. On the bristol board, draw 40 to 50 circles or other shapes. Draw interconnecting "paths" between the shapes.
2. Designate four START points; make one WINNER point ending the game.
3. In the remaining spaces, draw a symbol for a paw, a claw, and a hoof (or write the word).
4. Cover the gameboard with clear adhesive plastic.
5. Rule the folding bristol into at least thirty 2" squares. Paste an animal picture on each square.
6. Cover with clear adhesive plastic and cut apart into cards.

Playing the Game

This game is for two to four players.

1. Stack the cards face down on the gameboard.
2. Each player selects a START point and a game piece.
3. The first player takes a card from the stack; decides whether the animal on the card has paws, claws, or hooves; and moves a game piece along the path to a space marked with the animal's characteristic. The child can move the game piece in any direction to make a match, but only one player may occupy a space. (Note: Establish age-appropriate game rules to deal with this stipulation.)
4. The player places the card on the bottom of the pile.
5. Play continues. The first person to reach the end of the path wins the game.

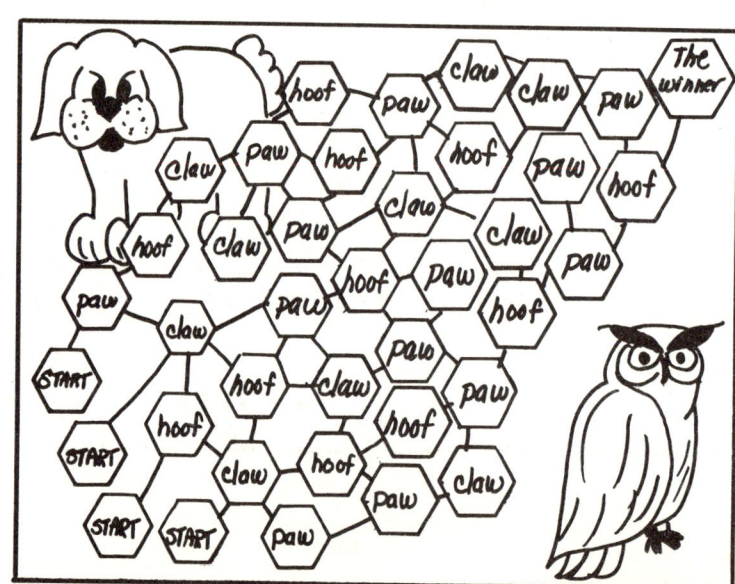

Exploring Living Things/Life Cycles of Animals ■ 87

WHICH CAME FIRST?

Directions to the teacher: Fold along the dotted line; reproduce the worksheet.
Discuss the life cycle of a butterfly and a frog.
Distribute the worksheets. Have the children color and cut out the pictures, and paste them according to life cycle sequence.

....

WHICH CAME FIRST?

Name _____   Date _____

Frog		Butterfly	
1.	2.	1.	2.
3.	4.	3.	4.

©1984 by Communication Skill Builders, Inc.
This page may be reproduced for instructional use.

88 ■ *Exploring Living Things/Environments of Animals*

SEARCH FOR ME

Objective
    To classify animals according to their environment

Materials
    Copies of the worksheet on page 89

Making the Game
    Reproduce the worksheet on page 89.

Playing the Game
1. Distribute copies of the worksheet.
2. Read the word list with the children.
3. Explain the game to the children. Read the directions aloud.
4. Have the children circle the animal words when they find them.

Exploring Living Things/Environments of Animals ■ 89

SEARCH FOR ME WORKSHEET

Name _____   Date _____

Draw a circle around the animal names.
The animals that live on the land will be found in the "land" section.
Those that live in the water will be found in the "water" section.
Those that fly through the air will be found in the "sky" section.

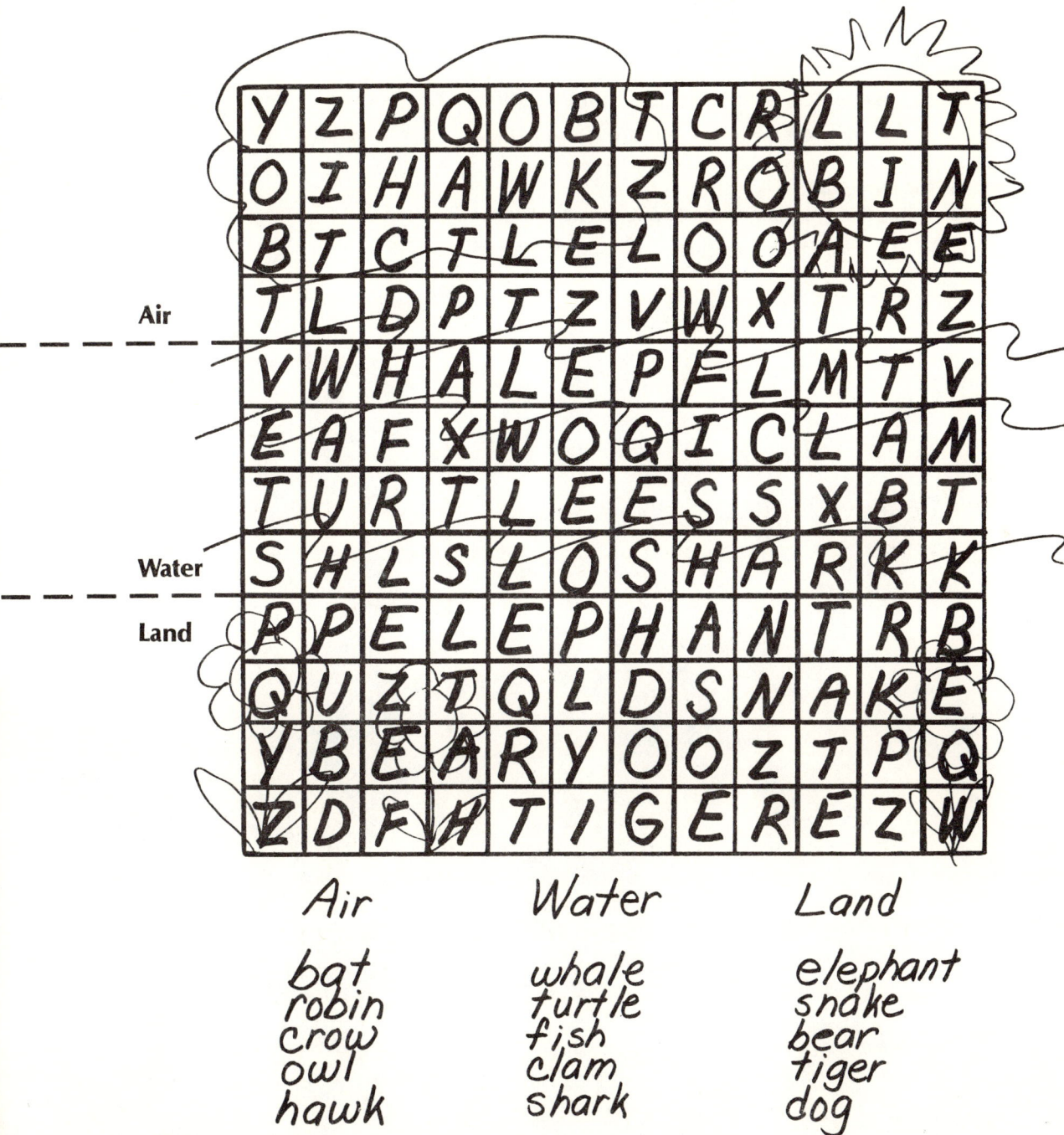

Y	Z	P	Q	O	B	T	C	R	L	T
O	I	H	A	W	K	Z	R	O	B	I N
B	T	C	T	L	E	L	O	O	A	E E
T	L	D	P	T	Z	V	W	X	T	R Z
V	W	H	A	L	E	P	F	L	M	T V
E	A	F	X	W	O	Q	I	C	L	A M
T	U	R	T	L	E	E	S	S	X	B T
S	H	L	S	L	O	S	H	A	R	K K
P	P	E	L	E	P	H	A	N	T	R B
Q	U	Z	T	Q	L	D	S	N	A	K E
Y	B	E	A	R	Y	O	O	Z	T	P Q
Z	D	F	H	T	I	G	E	R	E	Z W

Air — Water — Land (labels on left side of grid)

Air   Water   Land
bat   whale   elephant
robin   turtle   snake
crow   fish   bear
owl   clam   tiger
hawk   shark   dog

©1984 by Communication Skill Builders, Inc.
This page may be reproduced for instructional use.

HOW ARE THEY THE SAME?

Objective
To observe animal adaptations to their environment

Materials
Copies of the worksheet on page 91
Crayons
Scissors
Paste

Making the Game
Reproduce and distribute the worksheets.

Playing the Game
1. Have the children color and cut out the pictures at the bottom of the worksheet.
2. Have the children paste the pictures under the appropriate animal.

Questions for Discussion
1. How has the animal adapted to its environment?
2. How have humans copied the animal adaptation? Why?

Exploring Living Things/Environments of Animals ■ 91

HOW ARE THEY THE SAME?

Name _____ Date _____

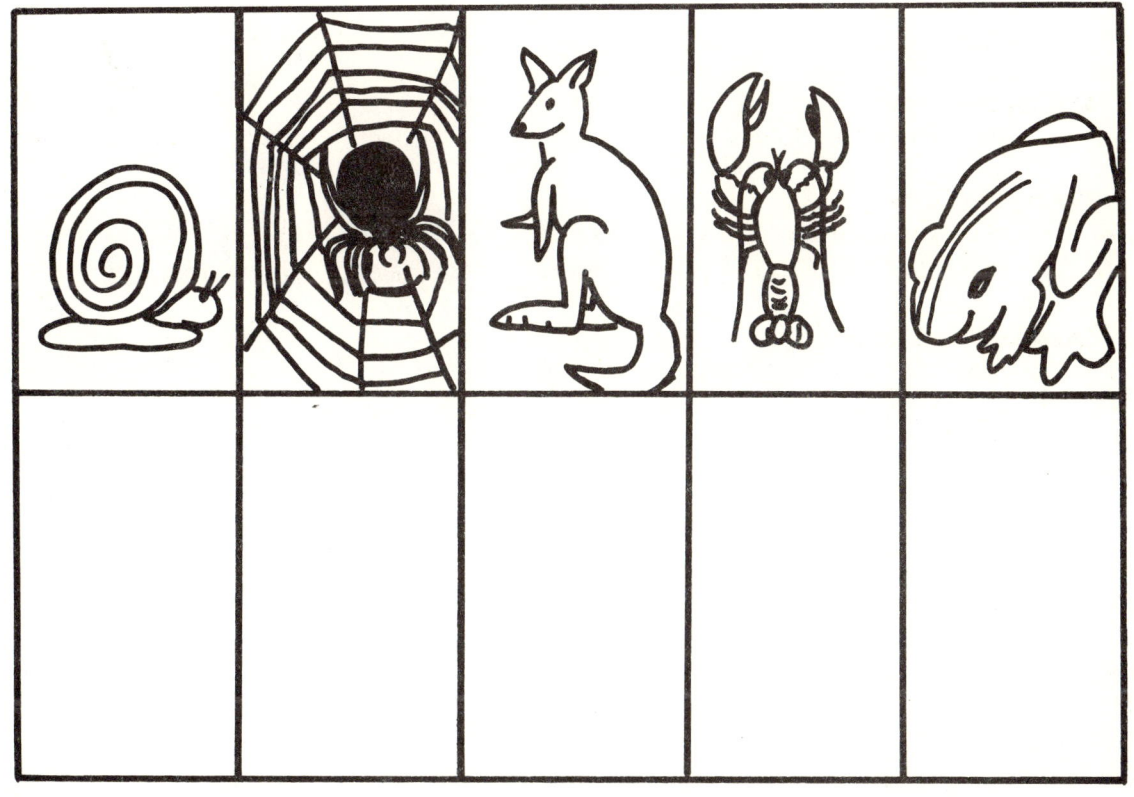

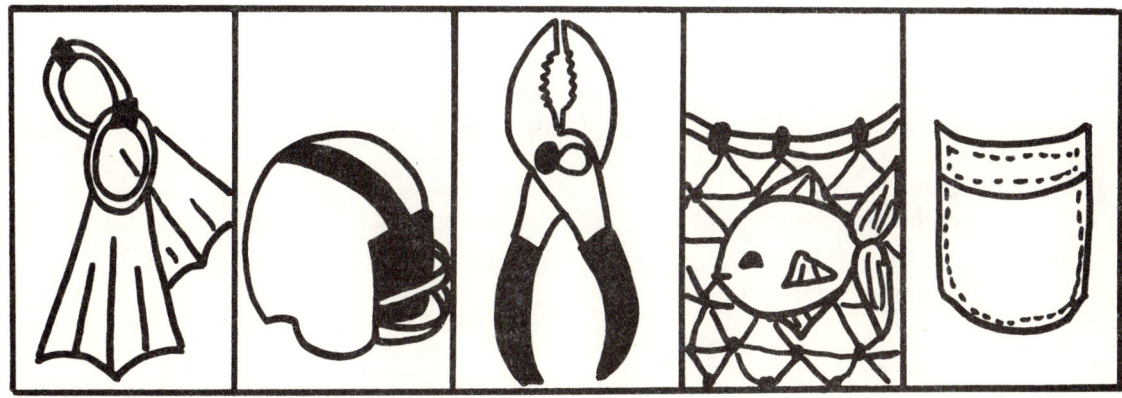

ANIMAL HOMES

Objective

To match animals and their habitat

Materials

Bristol board, 24" x 18" and three pieces each 2" x 3"

Folding bristol

Marking pens, ruler, scissors, paper punch, paste

3 paper fasteners

Drapery hooks

Clear adhesive plastic

Pictures of animals that live in trees, in water, or underground

Suggested Animals

Tree	Water	Underground
owl	tadpole	ant
squirrel	frog	snake
robin	turtle	rabbit
raccoon	fish	woodchuck
koala	otter	chipmunk
opossum	beaver	prairie dog

Making the Game

1. Rule the bristol board into three sections, each 8" wide.
2. On the bottom portion of each section, draw a tree, a pond, and a ground tunnel (see the illustration), representing animal habitats.
3. At the bottom of each section, draw a 2" x 3" rectangle. In it, write a list of animals that live in the habitat pictured above it.
4. Cover the board with clear adhesive plastic.
5. Cover the three 2" x 3" pieces of bristol board with clear adhesive plastic. Punch a hole in the top center of each piece. Cover each list of animals with one of the pieces, using paper fasteners to attach them to the board.
6. Place drapery hooks on the upper portion of the board.
7. Rule the folding bristol into 2" squares. On each square, paste a picture of an animal. Cover with clear adhesive plastic and cut apart into cards.

Playing the Game

1. The child sorts the cards according to the animals' habitats.
2. The child hangs the cards on the drapery hooks above the habitat, and checks the list under the cover to self-correct.

Exploring Living Things/Animals ■ 93

ANIMALS WORKSHEET

Name _____ Date _____

Cut out the pieces and paste them together.
What is this animal? Is it a pet?
What would you feed it?
Where would it live?
Read a book about this pet.

94 ■ *Exploring Living Things/Culminating Activity*

EXPLORING LIVING THINGS

Directions to the teacher: Fold along the dotted line; reproduce the worksheet.

Tell the children to read the clues, discover the word, and fill in the missing letters.

Answers: sun, calf, roots, rabbit, tadpole, elephant, woodchuck, watermelon

- -

EXPLORING LIVING THINGS

Name _____ Date _____

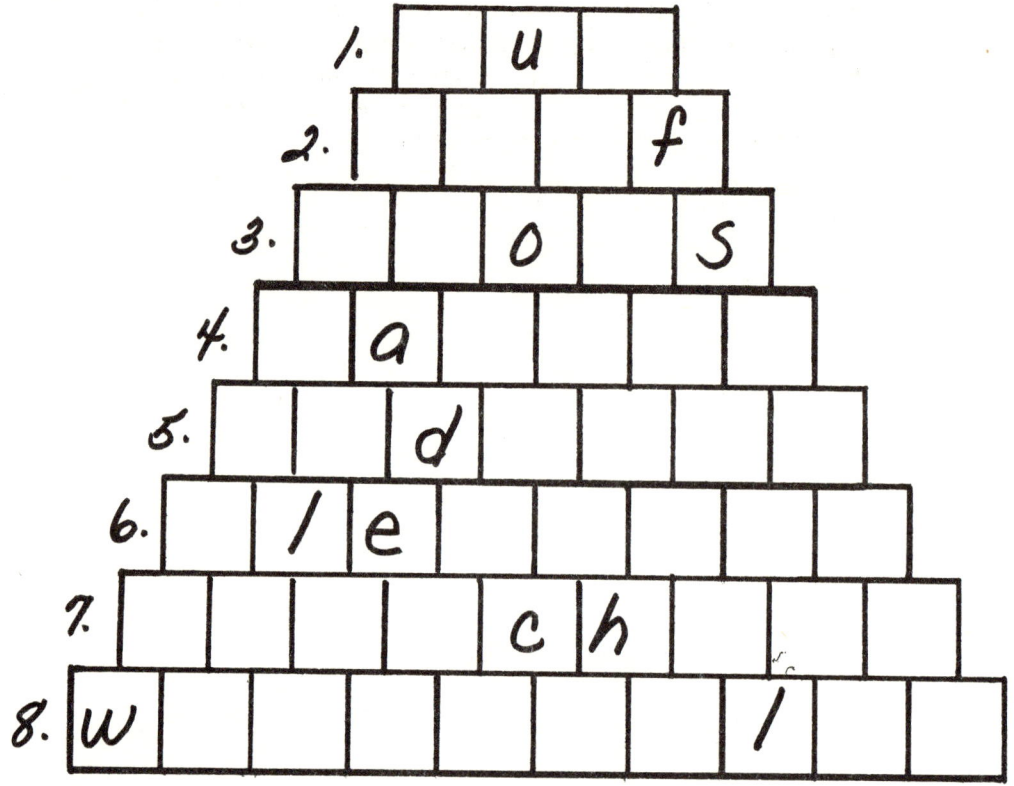

1. A plant needs this to grow
2. A baby cow
3. Always grows downward on a plant
4. Has long ears and likes carrots
5. A baby frog
6. A zoo animal
7. Lives underground
8. Fruit with black seeds

©1984 by Communication Skill Builders, Inc.
This page may be reproduced for instructional use.

Exploring the Environment

The activities in this unit are designed to alert the children to the basic need common to all living things. Ecology may not be fully understood by young children, but the seeds for preserving our environment must be planted in their minds, in order for our world to have a future.

The seasons, weather, water, and air are important because they affect our lives.

Seasons

Exploring the Environment/Observing the Seasons ■ 99

PRESERVE A BRANCH

Objective
To observe and compare leaves from a tree in the autumn and the spring

Materials
Autumn—A large jar
Glycerin
Water
A small branch with leaves that have just turned color
A hammer
A large container
Spring—A small branch from the same tree, with new leaves

Making the Game
Gather the materials.

Playing the Game
1. In a jar, mix one part glycerin to two parts water. (Add more solution later, if necessary.)
2. Pound the end of the branch until it is slightly crushed and feels soft.
3. Place the end of the branch in the glycerin. In about two weeks, the leaves will get thicker to the touch and the color will change slightly.
4. Place the preserved leaves in the large container. Keep them for classroom decoration.
5. In the spring, cut a branch from the same tree. Compare the spring leaves with the preserved branch.

ADOPT A TREE

Objective

To observe that a tree is affected by seasonal changes

Materials

September—A ribbon

April or May—Copies of the worksheet on page 101

Crayons, scissors, paste

Making the Game

Gather the materials.

Playing the Game

1. The class selects a tree that has a branch within reach. They tie the ribbon around the branch.
2. The children observe the branch during the four seasons. They draw and discuss what they observe each time they visit the tree.
3. In the springtime, copies of the worksheet are distributed. The children color the pictures, cut out the four season words, and paste them under the appropriate pictures.

Exploring the Environment/Observing the Seasons ■ 101

ADOPT A TREE

Name _____ Date _____

| spring | autumn | winter | summer |

Exploring the Environment/Observing the Seasons

PUMPKIN ACTIVITIES

Objective
To observe many uses for a pumpkin

Materials
Two green pumpkins (or more)
Marking pens
Spoon for scooping
Knife for carving
Cookie sheet
Salt, oil
Favorite pumpkin recipes
Soil
Small containers (one for each child)

Making the Game
1. In late September, obtain green pumpkins.
2. Gather the materials for each project, as needed.

Playing the Game
1. Observe the green pumpkins change color.
2. When the pumpkins are orange, close to Halloween, paint a face on one pumpkin. On the other, carve a jack-o'-lantern.
3. Separate the pumpkin seeds. Set aside some seeds for spring planting. Roast the remaining seeds for the class to eat.

   Roasted Pumpkin Seeds
   Spread seeds on a lightly oiled cookie sheet. Sprinkle with salt.
   Bake at 350° until brown, about 15 minutes.

4. After Halloween, use the jack-o'-lantern to make your favorite pumpkin cookies, bread, or pie.
5. In the spring, plant the pumpkin seeds in small containers. Have the children care for them in the classroom.
6. When the plants have sprouted, have the children take them home, plant them outside, and observe the pumpkin plant grow all summer.
7. The next Halloween, the children may carve their own homegrown pumpkins.

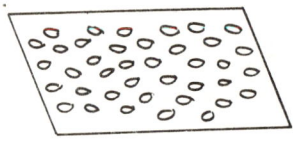
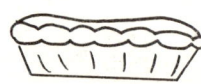

Exploring the Environment/Observing the Seasons ■ 103

LEAF ACTIVITIES

Objective
 To observe the structure of leaves

Materials
 Leaf rubbing— Leaves
  Newsprint
  Typing paper
  Stripped crayons
 Leaf stenciling— Leaves
  Drawing paper
  A small dish of poster paint
  A sponge
 Leaf printing— Leaves
  Bristol board, cut into leaf-sized pieces
  Glue
  A small dish of poster paint
  Typing paper

Making the Game
 Gather the materials and set up three art stations, as indicated above.

Playing the Game
 The children should move from station to station, completing each activity. Later, they should discuss their observations about the size, structure, and shape of the leaves.

 Leaf rubbing— The child places the leaf smooth side down on the newsprint, places a piece of typing paper over the leaf, and rubs the surface of the top paper with the stripped crayon. The veins and the shape of the leaf will appear on the paper.

 Leaf stenciling— The child places the leaf on a piece of drawing paper, dips the sponge into the poster paint, dabs or presses around the edge of the leaf with the sponge, and lifts away the leaf.

 Leaf printing— The child glues the top side of a leaf onto a piece of bristol board, coats the leaf with poster paint, places the leaf on a sheet of paper, and presses evenly all around the leaf.

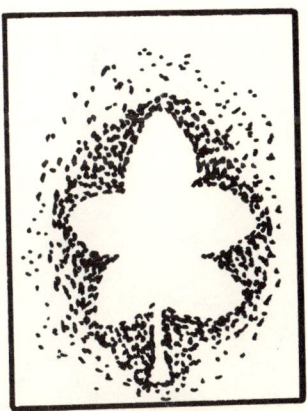

SNOW ART

Objective
To observe snowflakes

Materials
Snow
Dark cloth
Magnifying glass
Container
Soap flakes
Water
Dark paper

Making the Game
1. Collect the materials.
2. Make "snow" for the art activity below.

Modeling Snow
Mix 2 cups of soap flakes with water until it is thick enough to mold.

Playing the Game
1. Take the children outdoors during a light snowfall. Have them collect snowflakes on a piece of dark material, and observe the flakes through a magnifying glass.
2. Let the children play in the snow to observe how it feels (make snowmen and snow angels).
3. Fill a container with snow and bring it into the classroom. Have the children observe as the snow turns to water.
4. Have the children mold objects or make pictures by applying the soap flake mixture on dark paper, as a permanent reminder of their snow observations.

SPIN A SEASON

Objective
To recognize the seasons in which different types of clothing and tools can be used

Materials
A large pizza board
Bristol board
Marking pens, ruler, scissors, paste
Pictures of seasonal clothing and tools
Paper punch, paper fastener
Clear adhesive plastic

Making the Game
1. Following the illustration, divide the pizza board into four sections. Write the names of the four seasons and draw a 2½" x 3½" rectangle in each section. Cover the board with clear adhesive plastic.
2. Make a spinner from bristol board. Cover with plastic, punch a hole at one end, and attach it loosely to the center of the circle with a paper fastener.
3. Rule the bristol board into at least forty 2½" x 3½" sections. Draw or paste pictures of seasonal clothing or tools on the sections (for example, umbrella, mittens, rake, shovel, hose, hats, bathing suit, jacket). Duplicate some of the pictures. Cover with clear adhesive plastic and cut apart into cards.

Playing the Game
1. Shuffle the cards and distribute them evenly among the players.
2. The players place the cards face up.
3. The first player spins the spinner, chooses a picture card that matches the season, and explains how the item is used during the season. If the explanation is accepted, the player places the card on the board.
4. Play continues until a player places all cards on the pizza board. If a match can't be made, the player forfeits a turn.

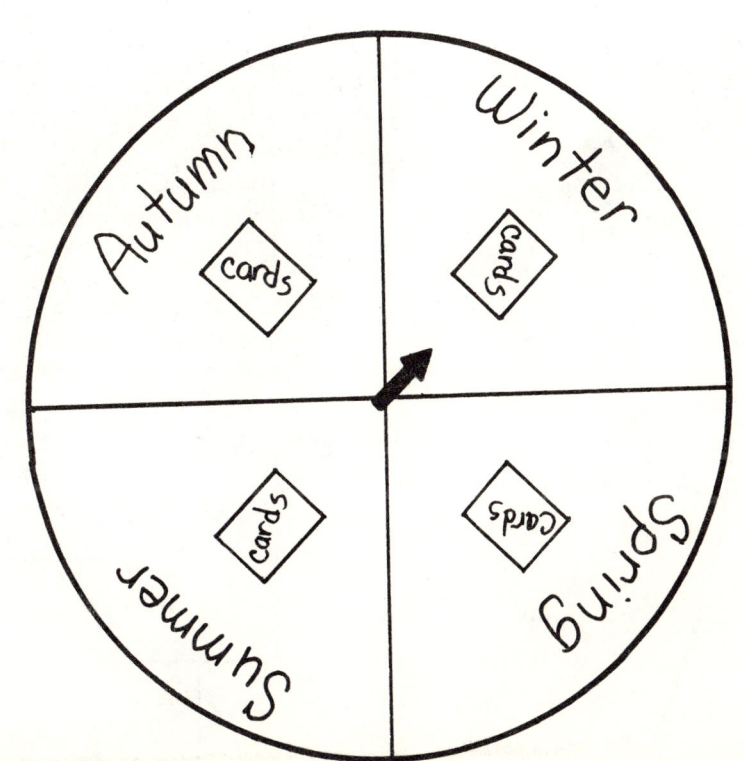

106 ■ *Exploring the Environment/Naming the Seasons*

THE SEASONS BULLETIN BOARD

Objective
    To recognize and name the months and holidays in each season

Materials
    Bristol board (dimensions according to need)
    Folding bristol
    Marking pens, ruler, scissors, paste
    Assorted seasonal and holiday symbols, stickers, and pictures
    Clear adhesive plastic
    Thumbtacks
    A date book obtained from a card shop
    Plastic bags

Making the Game
1. Divide the bristol board into four sections. Cover the board with clear adhesive plastic. Place it on the bulletin board near the classroom calendar.
2. Rule folding bristol into 2" squares. Cut and paste a holiday symbol or picture on each square. Cover with clear adhesive plastic and cut apart into cards.
3. Rule folding bristol into 12" x 3" sections. Write the names of the months and seasons on the strips. On the months that a season changes, make two strips and block out either the first or the last part of the month (see the illustration). Cover with clear adhesive plastic and cut the strips apart.
4. Thumbtack three plastic bags near the gameboards. Put the square cards in one bag, the strips in another, and the date book in the third bag.

Playing the Game
1. The child thumb-tacks the name of the season at the top of the board, and the months in the correct sequence.
2. The child selects appropriate seasonal and holiday cards and thumbtacks them to the board. (The date book may be used as a reference.)

To increase the difficulty, mix in more than one season's holidays.

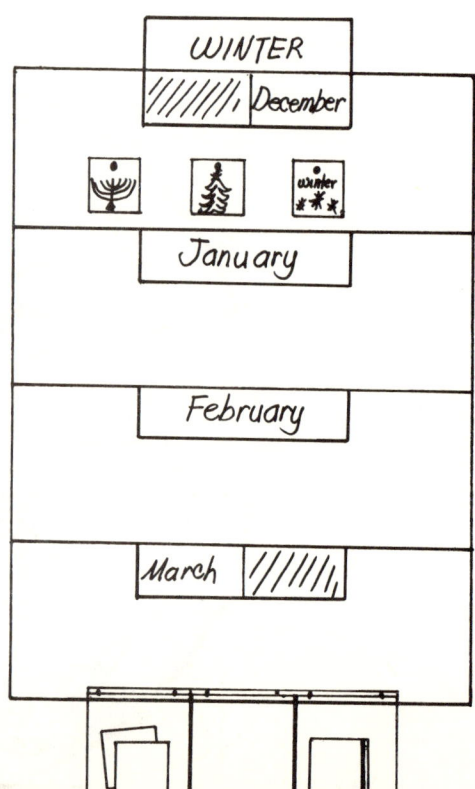

Exploring the Environment/Naming the Seasons ■ 107

GET ME HOME

Objective
To read and/or recognize seasonal words and symbols

Materials
Bristol board, 12" x 18" and a scrap piece
Marking pen, ruler, scissors
Paper punch, paper fastener
Clear adhesive plastic
Game pieces

Making the Game
1. Following the illustration, draw a four-way gameboard. Draw ten to twelve spaces on each branch leading to the goal HOME at the center of the tree.
2. Draw a 4" to 6" circle on the trunk of the tree. Divide it into four parts and write the names of the seasons in the spaces.
3. On each space on the board, draw a picture or write a word appropriate to one of the four seasons.
4. Cover the board with clear adhesive plastic.
5. Make a spinner from scrap bristol board. Cover with plastic, punch a hole at one end, and attach it loosely to the center of the circle with a paper fastener.

Playing the Game
This is a game for two to four players.
1. Each player selects a branch and places a game piece at START.
2. In order for the players to move out of the START square, they must spin a season to match the first picture on their branch.
3. The players spin in turn. Once the players are out of START, they may move their game pieces to the next space that matches the season spinner.
4. In order to win, a player must spin a season to match the last picture on the branch before that player can move into the hole in the tree.

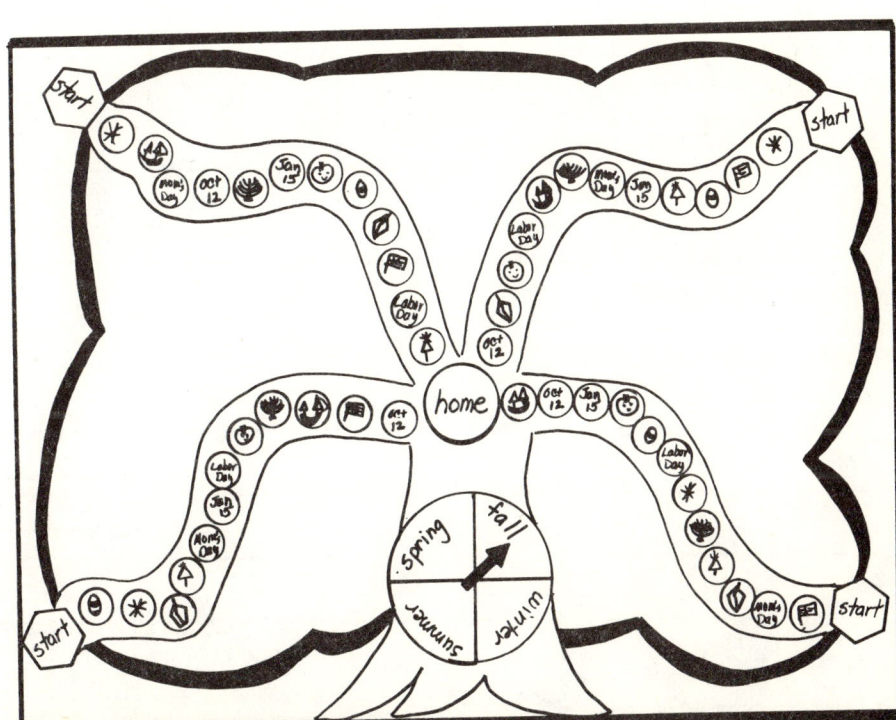

SEASONS WORKSHEET

Directions to the teacher: Fold along the dotted line; reproduce the worksheet.

Write a list of season words on the blackboard. Have each child construct a Find-a-Word, using **15** of the words. Have the children exchange their Find-a-Word puzzles and solve them.

....

SEASONS WORKSHEET

Name _____   Date _____

Water

FRESH WATER/SALT WATER

Objective
To observe the effect of salt in water

Materials
Water
Salt
2 large jars
4 glasses
A marking pen
6 labels
2 eggs
Food coloring
An eye dropper
2 ice cubes

Making the Game
Gather the materials.

Playing the Game
1. Fill the jars with water. Add salt to one jar. Label the jars FRESH WATER and SALT WATER. Put an egg in each jar. Observe what happens. Which egg rises?
2. Fill two glasses with water. Add salt to one glass. Label the glasses FRESH WATER and SALT WATER. Drop food coloring into each glass. Observe what happens.
3. Fill the remaining two glasses with water. Add salt to one glass. Label the glasses FRESH WATER and SALT WATER. Add an ice cube to each glass. Observe what happens. In which glass did the ice cube melt?
4. Discuss the effects of salt water.

WARM WATER/COLD WATER

Objective
>To understand that cold water is heavier than warm water

Materials
>A small aquarium
>A small bottle with a tight cap
>Food coloring
>Water

Making the Game
>Collect the materials.

Playing the Game
1. Fill the aquarium with very warm water. Fill the bottle with colored cold water. Cap the bottle and lower it sideways into the warm water. Remove the cap. The cold water will sink to the bottom of the tank.
2. Fill the aquarium with cold water. Fill the bottle with colored warm water. Cap the bottle and lower it sideways to the bottom of the aquarium. Remove the cap. Observe the warm water rise.

 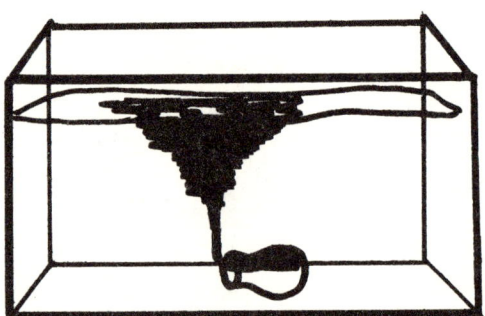

MAKE IT BIGGER

Objective
To observe that water magnifies objects

Materials
Plastic pail
Clear plastic wrap
Rubber band
Scissors

Making the Game
1. Cut a hole on each side of the plastic pail, large enough for a child to reach inside.
2. Cover the top of the pail loosely with plastic wrap. Secure it with a rubber band.
3. Pour water onto the top. (Experiment with different amounts of water.)

Playing the Game
The child holds objects through the holes to observe the effect of water.

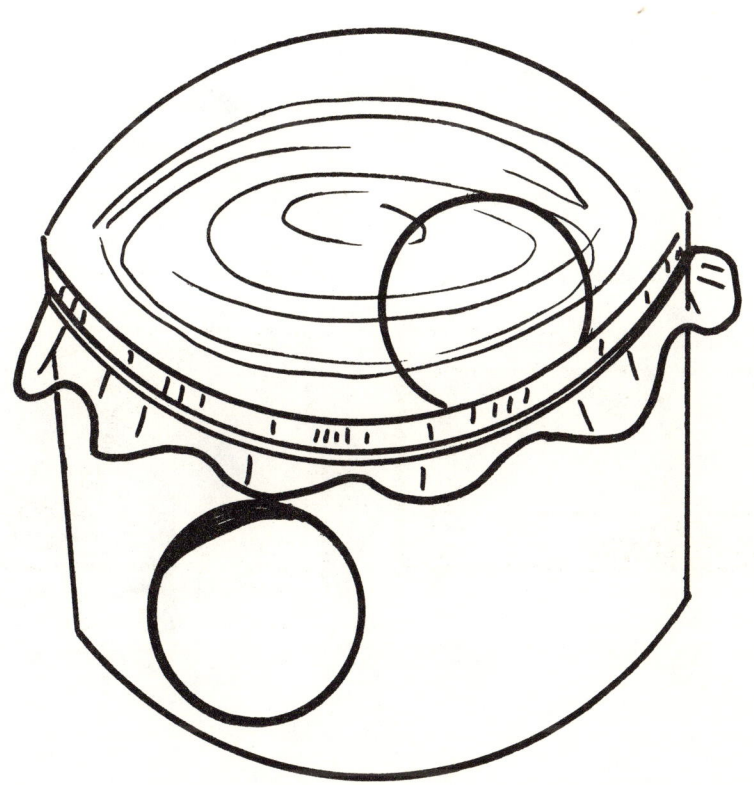

DISAPPEARING WATER

Objective
To understand that water can disappear into the air

Materials
A glass
A marking pen
Masking tape
Water
A sponge
A bowl

Making the Game
Gather the materials.

Playing the Game
1. Press a strip of masking tape vertically onto the glass. Fill the glass with water. Mark and date the water level. Observe and mark the water level daily.
2. Make two spots on the blackboard with a wet sponge. Cover one spot with the bowl. Observe the uncovered spot evaporate. When the water is gone, remove the bowl from the other spot.

Air gathers moisture and holds it invisibly. This is evaporation.

Questions for Discussion
1. Where did the water go?
2. Which spot had more air?

WATER FROM AIR

Objective
To understand that there is water vapor in the air

Materials
A large glass jar with a lid
Water
Food coloring
Ice cubes
Paper towels

Making the Game
Gather the materials.

Playing the Game
1. Wipe the jar with paper towels to show the children that it is dry.
2. Fill the jar with colored water and ice. Cover with the lid.
3. Allow the jar to sit at room temperature until water forms on the outside of the jar.
4. Wipe the jar with the paper towel to observe that the water is not colored and did not come from inside the jar.

Moisture condenses on cold surfaces.

Questions for Discussion
1. Where did the water come from?
2. What is all around the room and the jar?
3. Which is warmer, the jar or the air?

116 ■ *Exploring the Environment/Pollution*

EXPLORING UNDERWATER

Objective
> To observe objects underwater

Materials
> A half-gallon milk carton
> Scissors
> A clear plastic bag
> Rubber bands

Making the Game
1. Cut the top and bottom off the carton.
2. Use the rubber bands to hold the plastic smoothly and securely over one end.

Playing the Game
> Place the bottom of the carton into a stream or pond. Do not let the water go above the rubber bands. Observe pond or stream life.

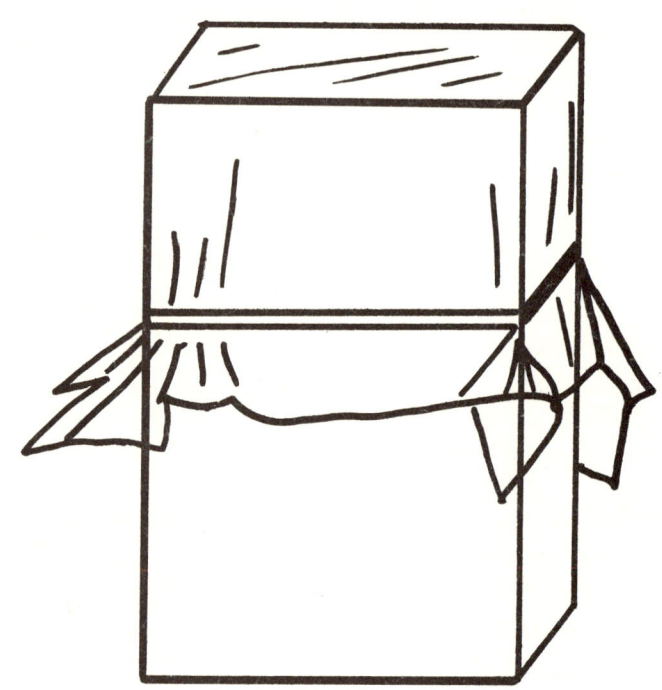

CLEAN IT UP

Objective
To understand how water becomes polluted

Materials
Two large jars with lids
Water
Detergents
Liquid fabric softener
Grease
Bleach

Making the Game
Collect the materials.

Playing the Game
1. Fill the jars halfway with water. In one jar, add detergent, fabric softener, grease, and bleach. Shake the jar. Observe both jars. Discuss which water the children would prefer to drink and wash in.

2. Experiment with different types of detergents in the jars to discover which makes the least amount of suds and therefore is the least polluting.

3. Discuss and make experience charts to list the things people can do to help stop polluting water.

CLEAN UP THE STREAM

Objective

To understand ways in which people can stop water pollution

Materials

Bristol board, 12" x 18"

Folding bristol

Marking pen, ruler, scissors

Clear adhesive plastic

Game pieces

A die

Making the Game

1. Following the illustration, draw the game on the bristol board. Cover with clear adhesive plastic.
2. Rule the folding bristol into thirty-six 2½" x 3¼" sections. On half, write positive ecology messages that correspond to your class discussions:

    Hooray! You threw your trash in the barrel! Move 4 spaces.
    You used a low sudsing detergent! Move 2 spaces.

    On the other half, write negative ecology messages:

    Shame! You used a colored tissue. Go back to START.
    Horrors! You left the water running. Lose a turn.

3. Cover with clear adhesive plastic and cut apart into cards.

Playing the Game

1. The players take turns rolling the die and moving their game pieces the number of spaces indicated.
2. A player lands on a bridge, draws a card, and follows the directions.
3. The first player to reach the end wins the game.

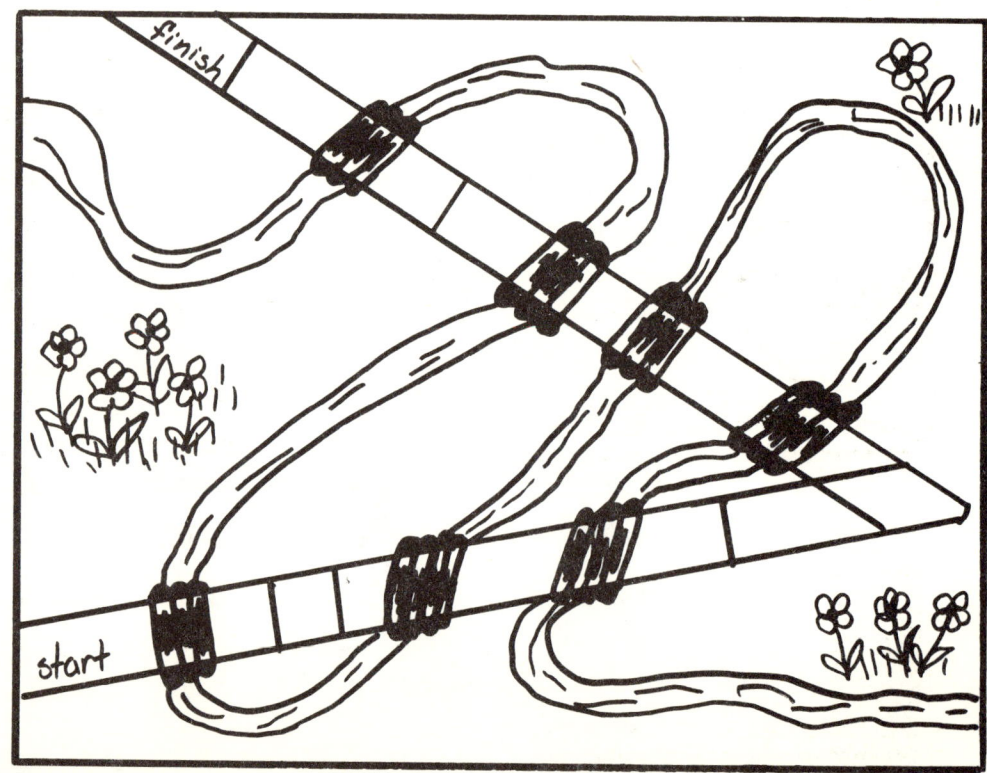

WATER WORKSHEET

Name _____ Date _____

Color the polluting word spaces RED.
Color the nonpolluting natural word spaces GREEN.

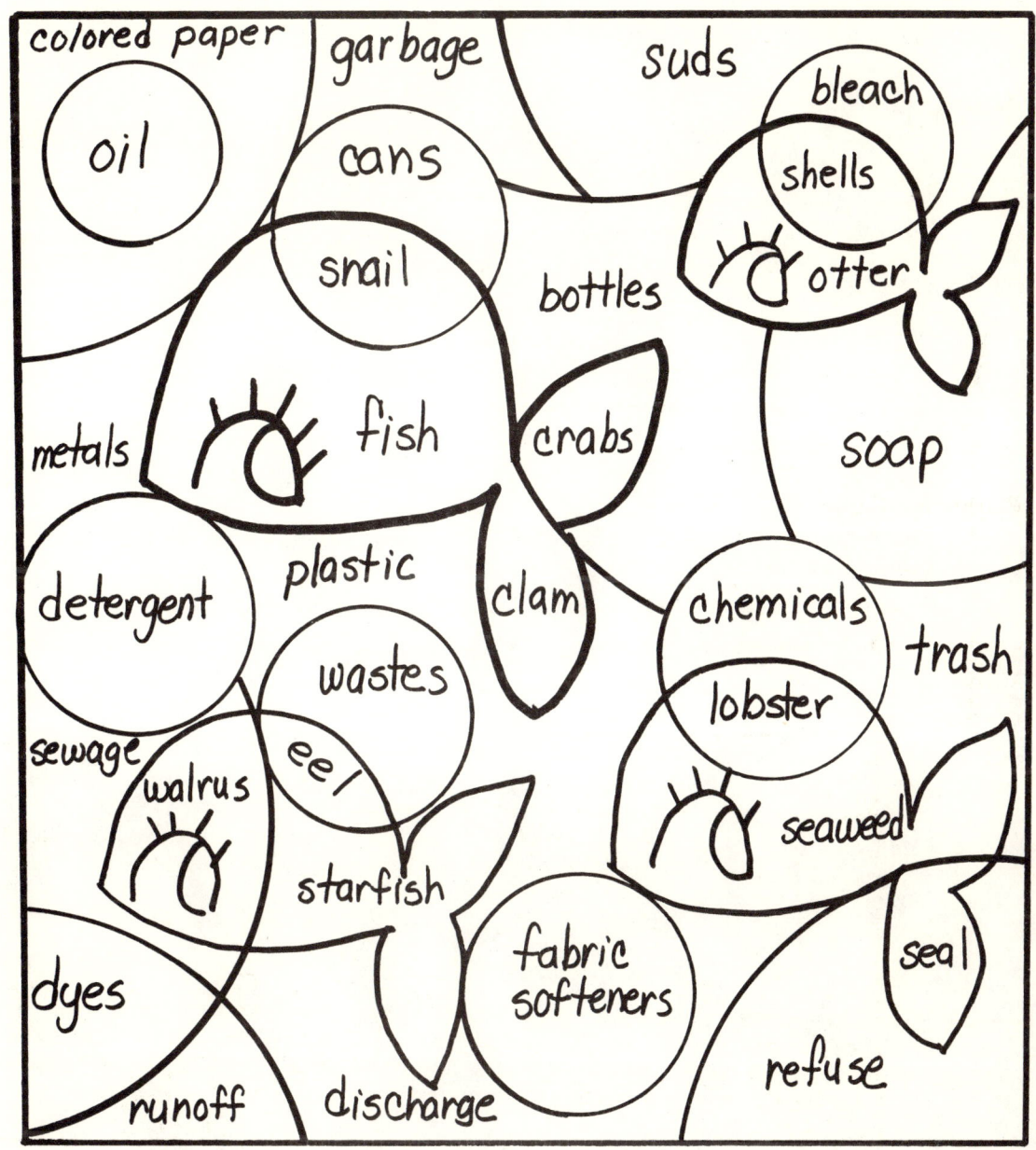

Air

IS IT THERE?

Objective
To understand that air exists even though it is not visible

Materials
A soft, clear plastic bottle
A balloon
Plastic sandwich bags

Making the Game
Gather the materials.

Playing the Game
1. Show the bottle to the children. Discuss whether it is empty. Squeeze the bottle near a child's face. Discuss what is felt coming out of the bottle.
2. Have the children watch as you blow up the balloon. Let them feel the filled balloon. Allow a child to feel the air escape. Discuss what escaped. (Did the children see it?)
3. Give each child a plastic bag. Have them capture air. Allow the children to feel the filled bag. Then have them squeeze the bag to let the air out.

Questions to Discuss
1. Is air all around us?
2. Can we see it?

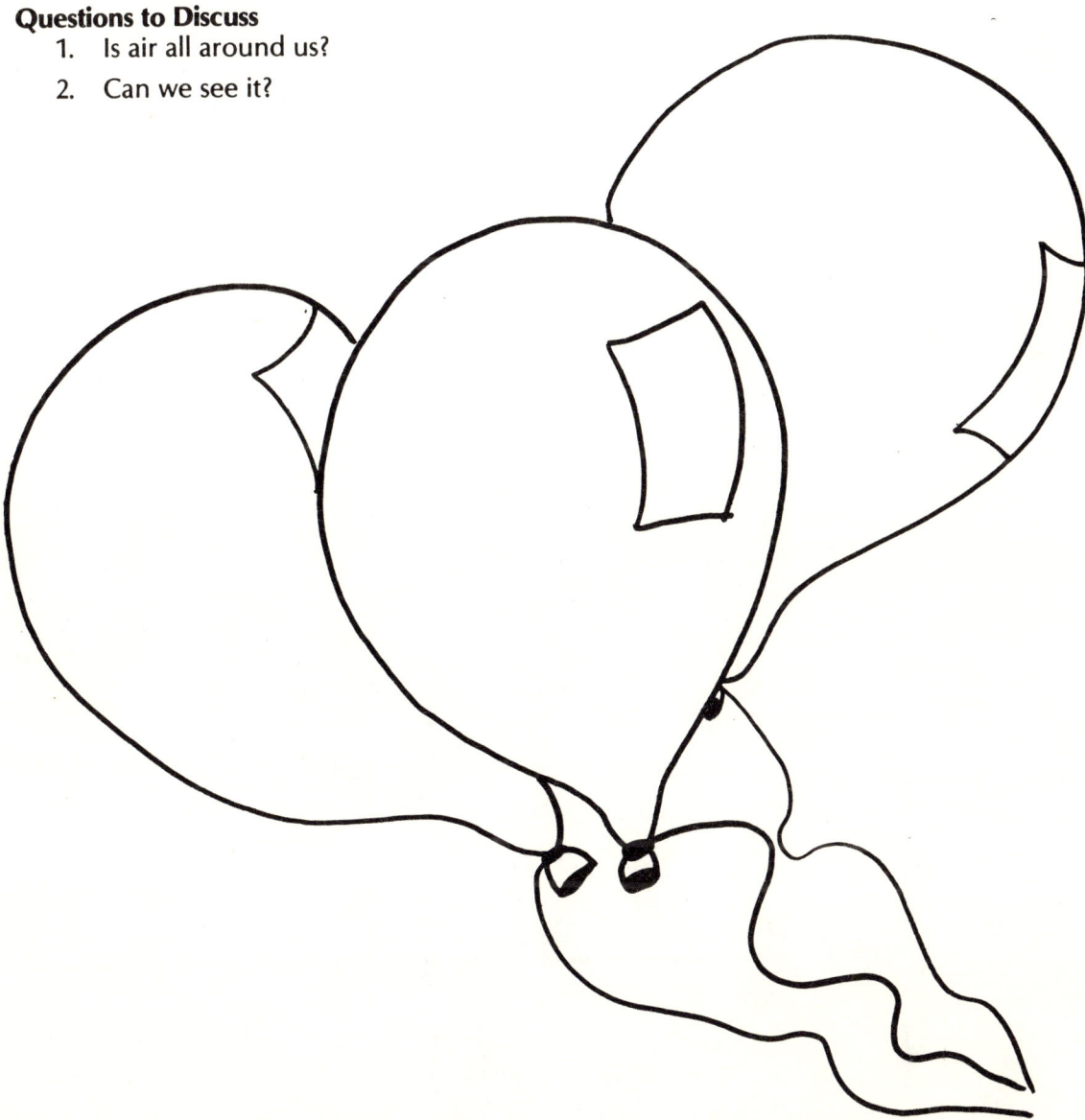

BURN OUT

Objective
To understand that air is necessary for a flame to burn

Materials
Two candles
Matches
A large drinking glass

Making the Game
Collect the materials.

Playing the Game
1. Review the discussion and conclusions reached in the "Is It There?" activity.
2. Light both candles.
3. Place the glass over one lighted candle.

Questions for Discussion
1. Which candle had the most air around it?
2. What happened to the air in the glass. Why?

DON'T GET WET

Objective
To understand that air takes up space

Materials
A drinking glass

Paper

Aquarium or large clear container filled with water

Making the Game
Collect the materials.

Playing the Game
1. Discuss from previous experiments whether there is air in the glass.
2. Wad up the paper in the glass. Turn the glass upside down, making sure it is level. Lower it into the water.
3. Lift the glass out of the water carefully. Show that the paper is still dry. The air has kept the water out.
4. Lower the glass into the water again. Tilt the glass. The children will observe the air escaping in bubbles.

Questions for Discussion
1. Why was the paper dry the first time?
2. What was in the bubbles?

STRAW PAINTING

Objective
To understand that air can move objects

Materials
White drawing paper
Thin poster paints
Drinking straws

Making the Game
Gather the materials.

Playing the Game
1. Dribble poster paint onto the drawing paper.
2. Have each child use a straw to blow the paint around the drawing paper, making a design.

Use several colors to make an interesting picture.

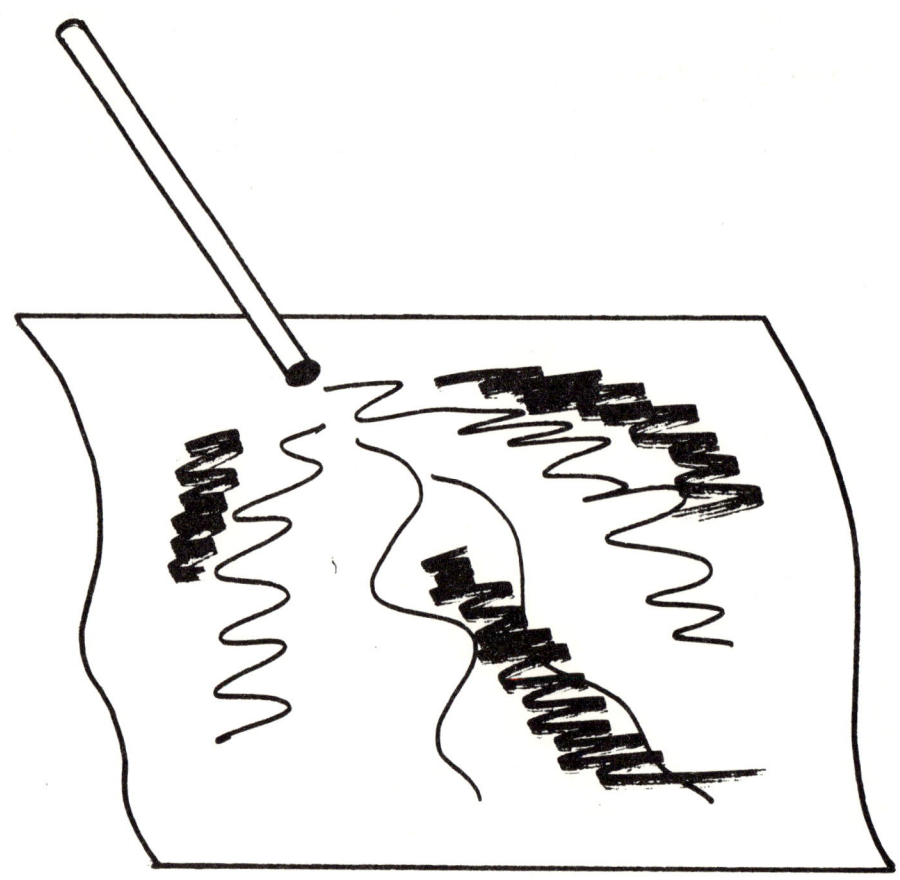

ADD-A-STRAW

Objective
To demonstrate that air can move water

Materials
A soft-drink bottle
Water
Drinking straws
Clay
Tape

Making the Game
1. Collect the materials.
2. Fill the bottle with water.

Playing the Game
1. Put a straw in the bottle. Mold clay around the straw at the top of the bottle, to make a cork. The child tries to suck up the water. (The clay keeps the air pressure away from the water.)
2. Remove the clay. The child sucks the straw. The air pressure on the water pushes it up the straw.
3. Tape straws together to see how many straws high the water will move.

Questions for Discussion
1. In the first experiment, what kept the water from coming up the straw?
2. In the second experiment, what pushed the water up the straw?

FUN WITH AIR

Objective
To understand that air can move objects

Materials
A kite and string
Copies of the pinwheel pattern on page 129
Scissors
A stapler
½" brads
Wooden clothespins (not spring-type)
A hammer
Construction paper
Corks
Toothpicks
Glue
A marking pen
A dishpan of water

Making the Game
1. Assemble the kite.
2. Reproduce the pinwheel pattern and instructions for each child.
3. Make flags for the corks by gluing small triangles of paper to the toothpicks. Stick the toothpicks into the corks. Label them 1, 2, 3, and so on.
4. Set up two stations—one for making pinwheels, another for cork races.

Playing the Game
Have a parent or an aide help with these activities.
Divide the class into three groups.
1. One group will go outdoors to fly the kite, supervised by an adult.
2. The second group will make pinwheels, following the directions on the pattern.
3. The third group will race the corks. Place the corks in the dishpan of water. The children will blow on the corks to move them over the water.

FUN WITH AIR: Making a Pinwheel

1. Cut out the square.
2. Cut along the dotted lines. Stop at the circle.
3. Bring the numbered points to the X in the center. Do not fold.
4. Staple the points to the center.
5. Push a brad into the center, close to the staple. Hammer the brad to the top of a clothespin. Leave the brad raised slightly so the pinwheel will spin.

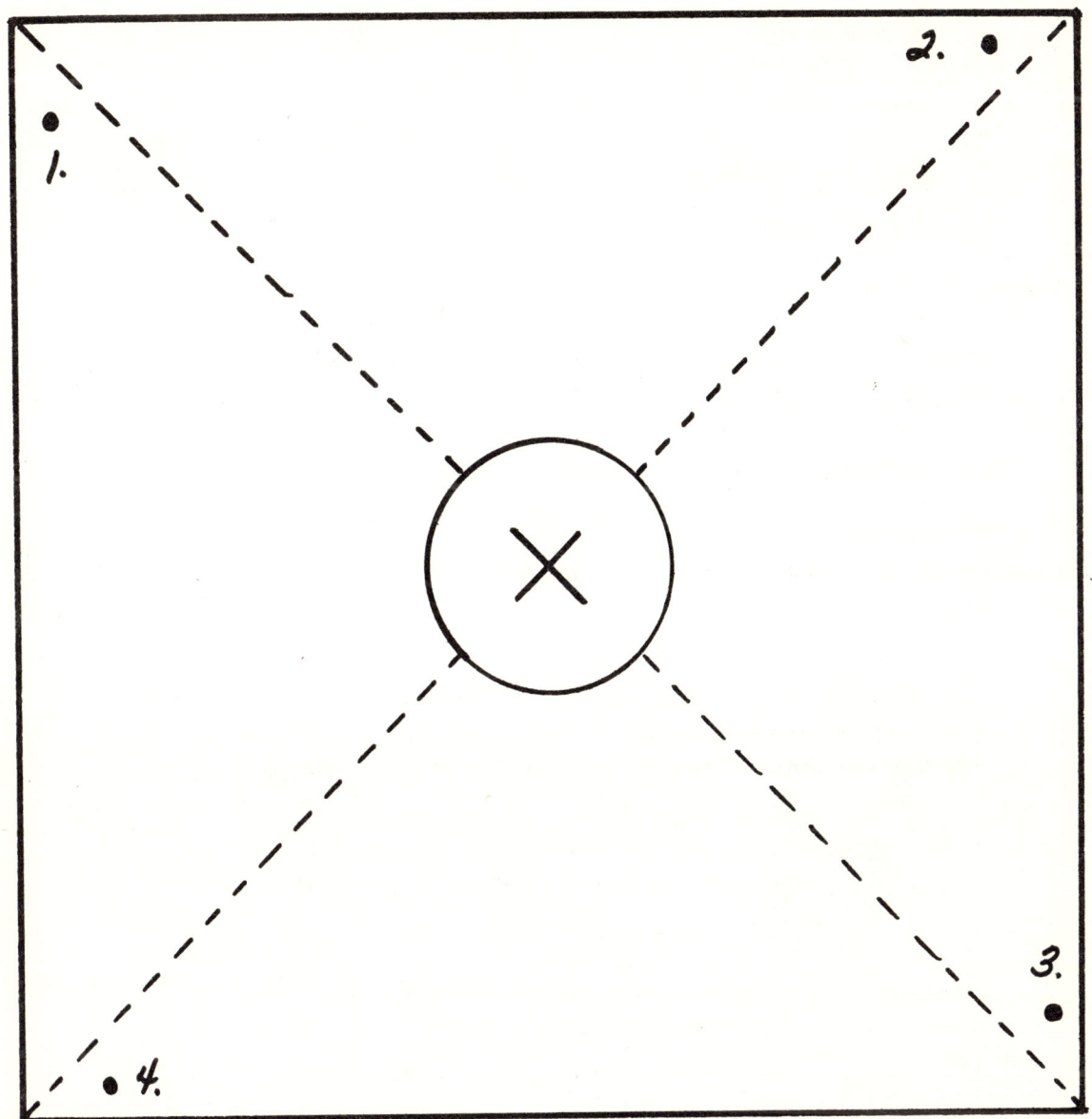

©1984 by Communication Skill Builders, Inc.
This page may be reproduced for instructional use.

NORTH, EAST, SOUTH, OR WEST?

Objective

To understand the directional terms used with a weather vane

Materials

Bristol board, 18" x 24" and a scrap piece

Marking pen, ruler, scissors

Clear adhesive plastic

Paper punch, paper fastener

A blank die

Game pieces

Making the Game

1. Rule the bristol board into 1" squares (see the illustration), eighteen across and eighteen down.
2. In the center of the board, make a 4" circle. Divide the circle into eight pie shapes. Label the circle as the points of the compass.
3. In four squares around the circle, mark a star to indicate START points.
4. Label the edges of the board with compass directions and draw arrows at each point (see the illustration).
5. Cover the board with clear adhesive plastic.
6. Make a spinner from bristol board. Cover with plastic, punch a hole at one end, and attach it loosely to the center of the circle with a paper fastener.
7. Using each number twice, write numbers 1, 2, or 3 on the die.

Playing the Game

This is a game for four players.

1. Each player places a game piece in one of the starred spaces.
2. The players take turns spinning the spinner to find out which direction to move, then rolling the die to find out how many spaces to move in that direction. (Northeast, southeast, southwest, and northwest are diagonal moves.)
3. The first player to move off the board wins the game.

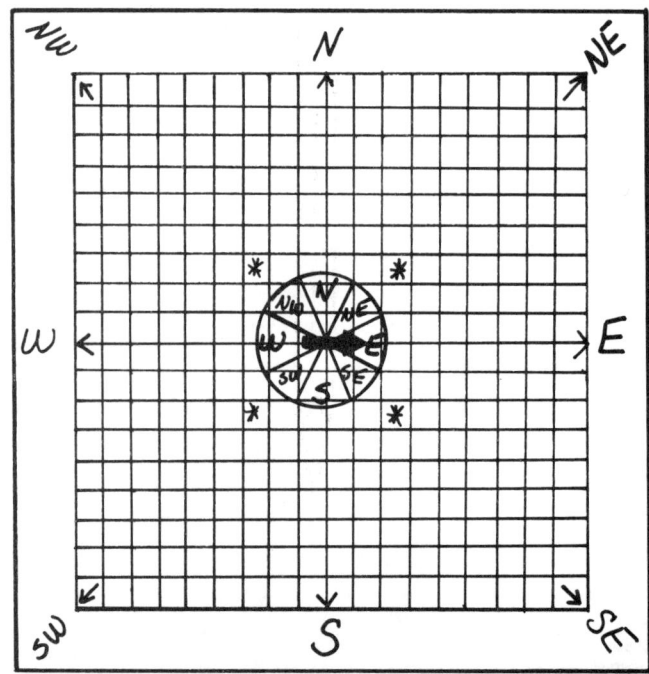

WHICH WAY?

Objective
To find the direction of the wind

Materials
Bristol board
Scissors, glue
A drinking straw
A straight pin
Pencil

Making the Game
1. Cut two arrow tails and points from the bristol board. (The tails must be larger than the points.) Glue the identical pieces together (for double thickness) at either end of the straw.
2. Stick a pin through the straw into the top of the eraser on the pencil (see the illustration).

Playing the Game
1. Take the weather vane outdoors.
2. Draw a circle on the ground. Mark the directions N, S, E, W.
3. The children take turns standing in the circle, holding the weather vane. The arrow should point into the wind. If the arrow points to E, the wind is coming from the east.

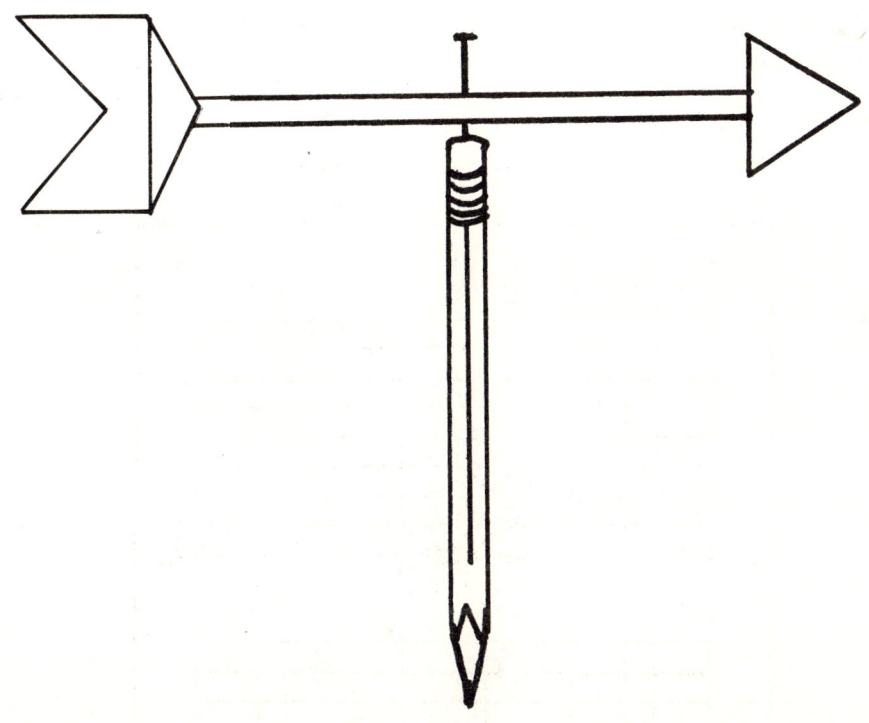

132 ■ *Exploring the Environment/Air*

AIR WORKSHEET

Directions to the teacher: Fold along the dotted line; reproduce the worksheet.

Have the children cut out the happy and sad faces and paste them in place as directed on the worksheet.

Answers: True—2, 4, 6, 9, 10   False—1, 3, 5, 7, 8

AIR WORKSHEET

Name _____   Date _____

Cut out the HAPPY and SAD faces.
Read the questions. Decide if the statement is true or false.
If the answer is TRUE, paste in a HAPPY face.
If the answer is FALSE, paste in a SAD face.

1. If the weather vane points to the North the wind is coming from the South.
2. The wind can move seeds.
3. Air cannot lift water.
4. There is air in soil.
5. A candle can burn without air.
6. Air is all around us.
7. Only people need air to live.
8. We can see air.
9. A weather vane helps to find the direction of the wind.
10. Air pushes water up a straw.

©1984 by Communication Skill Builders, Inc.
This page may be reproduced for instructional use.

Weather

BLOW IT UP

Objective
To observe that air expands when heated

Materials
A balloon
A small bottle
A pan
Warm water

Making the Game
Gather the materials.

Playing the Game
1. Snap the balloon over the neck of the bottle.
2. Place the bottle in the pan of warm water.
3. Observe what happens.

Questions for Discussion
1. What happens to the balloon?
2. What is in the jar?
3. What happens to the air in the jar?

THE THERMOMETER

Objective
>To understand how a thermometer works

Materials
>A thermometer
>Bowls of hot and cold water
>A slender glass tube
>Red colored water
>A marking pen
>A candle, matches
>A bowl of ice cubes

Making the Game
>Collect the materials

Playing the Game
1. Experiment with a thermometer. Observe and discuss what happens when it is placed in a bowl of warm water and a bowl of cold water.
2. Fill the slender tube half-full of colored water. Mark the level of the water. Hold the tube over a lighted candle. Observe the level of the water rise slightly above the mark.
3. After the tube is cool, place it in a bowl of ice cubes. Observe whether the level lowers.

Refer to "Blow It Up," the experiment that shows air expands when heated.

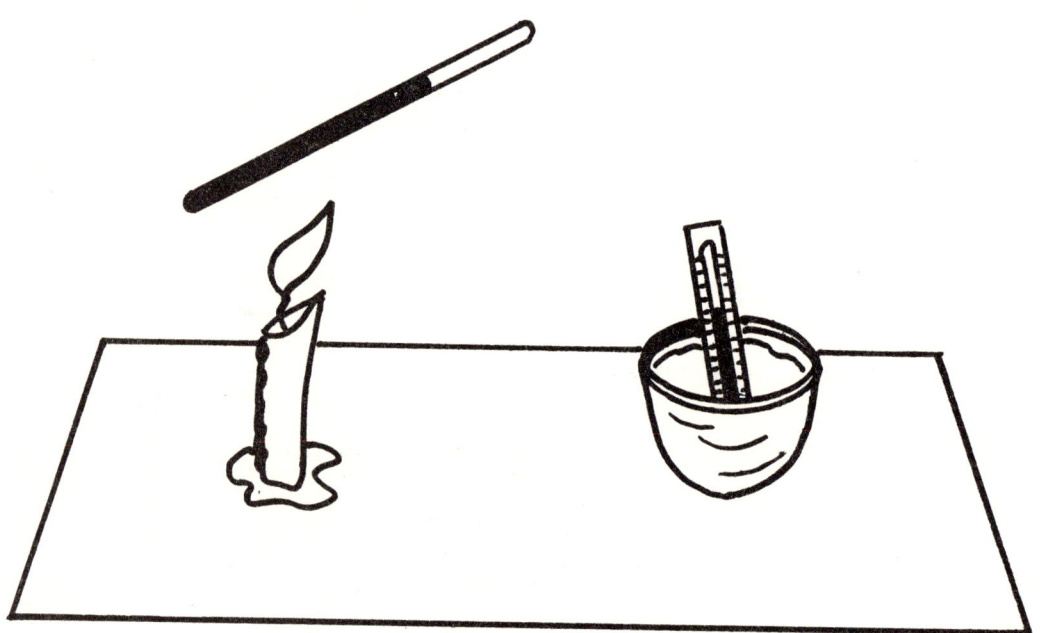

A BAROMETER

Objective
To make an instrument to measure air pressure

Materials
- A peanut butter jar
- A balloon
- Scissors
- An elastic band
- A drinking straw
- Tape
- Paper
- Marking pen

Making the Game
1. Cut a piece of the balloon and stretch it tightly across the top of the jar. Hold it in place with the elastic band.
2. Cut the end of the straw diagonally to make a pointer. Fasten the other end of the straw to the center of the balloon surface with a piece of tape.
3. Following the illustration, make a weather chart on paper. Write WEATHER CONDITIONS, HIGH, and LOW on the chart (high indicates fair weather and low indicates stormy). Tape the chart to a wall.

Playing the Game
1. Place the barometer close to but not touching the chart.
2. Check the weather daily for a week. Mark the chart next to the pointer and write the weather condition.
3. Every time the pointer moves during the day, mark the chart again and write the weather condition.

As the pressure of the air increases, it pushes the surface of the balloon downward, causing the pointer to move upward. When the air pressure is low, the normal pressure in the bottle pushes up, causing the pointer to dip down.

Questions for Discussion
1. What kind of weather is occurring when the pointer is near HIGH?
2. What kind of weather is occurring when the pointer is near LOW?
3. What makes the pointer move?

WEATHER RECORD

Objective
>To observe weather conditions

Materials
>Copies of the worksheet on page 139
>Pencils, crayons

Making the Game
>Reproduce and distribute the worksheets.

Playing the Game
1. Discuss the various weather conditions designated on the worksheet.
2. Decide on a number of days in which the children will observe the weather.
3. Tell the children that each one is responsible for making checkmarks on the worksheet to record daily weather conditions.
4. At the end of the time period, each child totals the number of checks in each weather column. The children then compare their lists with those of the other children.

Exploring the Environment/Weather Terms ■ 139

WEATHER RECORD CHECKLIST

Name _____   Date _____

Record the weather for each day in the correct columns. Some days will have a variety of weather conditions.

WEATHER RECORD					
sunny	rain	cloudy	windy	snow	partly sunny
total	total	total	total	total	total

© 1984 by Communication Skill Builders, Inc.
This page may be reproduced for instructional use.

MAKING FOG

Objective
To understand what causes fog

Materials
A jar
A cup of hot water
Ice cubes

Making the Game
Gather the materials.

Playing the Game
1. Pour a cup of hot water into the jar.
2. Place an ice cube on the jar opening.
3. Place the jar where the children can see light shining through it.
4. Observe what happens inside the jar.

When moist cold air and warm air meet, fog is formed.

Question for Discussion
What happens when the warm air comes up to meet the ice?

WEATHER WATCH

Objective
To understand weather terms

Materials
Bristol board
Marking pens, ruler, scissors or paper cutter
Clear adhesive plastic
Game pieces
A die

Making the Game
1. Rule the bristol board into about forty 3" square cards.
2. Write directions on most of the cards. Include:

START	TAKE AN EXTRA TURN
WINNER	MOVE BACK 1 SPACE
FREE SPACE	MOVE FORWARD 3 SPACES
LOSE A TURN	MOVE BACKWARD 2 SPACES

   On the remaining cards, draw pictures to match some of the directions (for example, write IT'S SNOWY! MOVE TO THE MITTENS, and draw mittens on a card).
3. Cover with clear adhesive plastic and cut apart into cards.

Playing the Game
1. Remove the START and WINNER cards. Shuffle the deck.
2. Lay out the cards as illustrated. (The path pattern will vary from game to game!) Place the START and WINNER cards at the beginning and end of the path.
3. The first player rolls the die, moves a game piece the number of spaces indicated, and follows the direction written on the card.
4. Play continues, with each player taking a turn until a child reaches the end.

MEASURE THE WIND

Objective
 To understand that winds can be classified according to velocity

Materials
 Bristol board, two large pieces
 Folding bristol
 Marking pen, ruler, scissors
 Clear adhesive plastic
 Game pieces

Making the Game

1. In the classroom, discuss some of the things that can occur when different types of winds blow. Make a Wind Chart, listing the information on a piece of bristol board. Some of the effects of wind might be:

Breeze	**Gale**	**Storm**
Wind vanes show the wind path	Trees bend over	Trees blow over
Twigs and leaves blow around	Twigs break off trees	Branches break off trees
Seeds blow away	Papers blow away	Wires fall
Dust blows around	It's hard to walk	Windows break
Kites fly	Things blow off the roof	Roofs blow away
Sailboats move	Umbrellas blow inside out	Umbrellas blow away

2. Draw a path on the bristol board, following the illustration. Randomly mark the terms BREEZE, GALE, and STORM. Decorate the gameboard. Cover with clear adhesive plastic.

3. Rule the folding bristol into 2" x 3" sections. On each section, write an effect of wind, using information from the Wind Chart. Cover with clear adhesive plastic and cut apart into cards.

Playing the Game

1. Stack the phrase cards face down on the gameboard.

2. The first player picks up the top card, reads the phrase aloud, and moves a game piece to the nearest appropriate wind description.

3. If all players agree that the wind description is correct, play continues. If there is a question or challenge, the players refer to the Wind Chart.

4. The first player to reach the finish line wins the game.

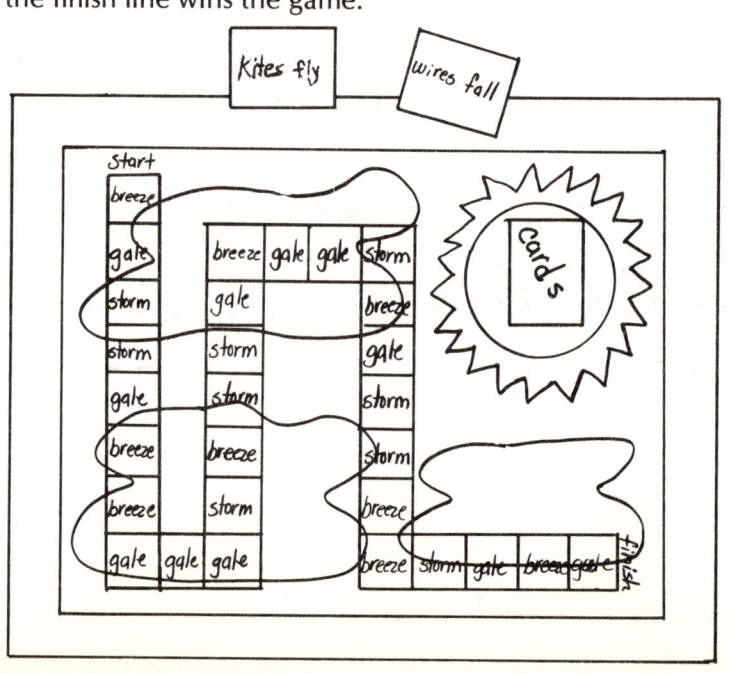

FIND THE MYSTERY WEATHER WORD

Name _____ Date _____

Down
1. A train runs on a _ a i _ road track.
2. Look at the _ a i _ boat.
3. Put sand in the _ a i _.
4. The hammer hits the _ a i _.

Across
1. The weather word is _ _ _ _.

Down
1. In school we have _ _ o w and tell.
2. I _ _ o w the answer.
3. A _ _ o w is a black bird.
4. I can _ _ _ o w the ball.

Across
1. The weather word is _ _ _ _.

WEATHER WORKSHEET

Name _____ Date _____

Use the alphabet code to answer the questions. Match the numbers to the letters.

Use the code to make up your own questions. Then trade them with a classmate to solve.

A	B	C	D	E	F	G	H	I	J	K	L	M	N
1	2	3	4	5	6	7	8	9	10	11	12	13	14

O	P	Q	R	S	T	U	V	W	X	Y	Z
15	16	17	18	19	20	21	22	23	24	25	26

1. This measures air pressure
   __ __ __ __ __ __ __ __ __
   2 1 18 15 13 5 20 5 18

2. This wind blows umbrellas inside out.
   __ __ __ __
   7 1 12 5

3. This is formed when moist air and cold air meet.
   __ __ __
   6 15 7

4. This tells us the temperature.
   __ __ __ __ __ __ __ __ __ __
   20 8 5 18 13 15 13 5 20 5 18

5. It happens when air pressure is low.
   __ __ __ __ __
   19 20 15 18 13

EXPLORING THE ENVIRONMENT

Name _____ Date _____

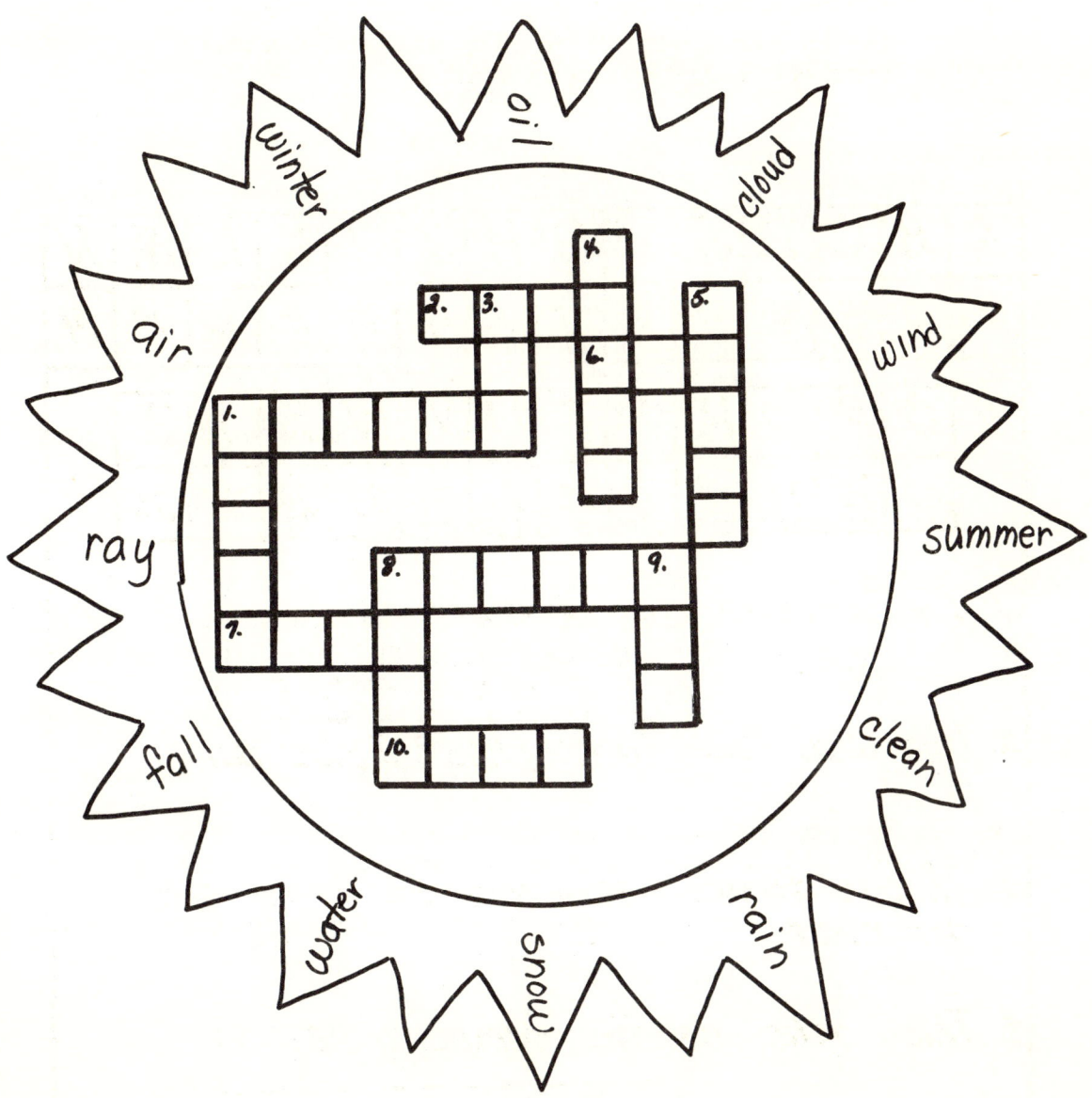

ACROSS
1. Snow time
2. Autumn
6. Good for salad, bad for the ocean
7. Drops from fluffy water holders
8. Season following Spring
10. Moving air

DOWN
1. We drink it
3. We breathe it
4. Fluffy water holder
5. Not dirty
8. Frozen rain
9. A beam of sunlight

More titles by Trudy Aarons and Francine Koelsch . . .

101 READING ACTIVITIES (1983)
This activity book offers you a systematic way to deal with the problems of the "not-ready-to-read" child. Provide your students with games in seven skill areas: sequencing, clozure, rhyming, alphabet, sight vocabulary, logos, and phonics. Each section includes a pre/post-test and reproducible follow-up worksheets. **Catalog No. 2079-Y $11.95**

101 MATH ACTIVITIES (1981)
You needn't be artistic to turn basic materials into effective, eye-catching games for math. Here are instructions for games in these skill categories: classification, ordering, counting, numbers, joining sets, and measurement. **Catalog No. 2065-Y $11.95**

101 LANGUAGE ARTS ACTIVITIES (1979)
This popular manual presents game ideas in 12 learning areas. These include visual discrimination and memory, auditory discrimination and memory, classification, seriation, spatial, motor, and more. Each activity is easy to make and inexpensive!
 Catalog No. 3053-Y $11.95

Other enriching materials from Communication Skill Builders . . .

SCRATCH 'N SNIFF LABELS
These full-color stickers are pressure-sensitive and contain encapsulated aromas of nine different foods—pizza, pickle, chocolate, orange, lemon, strawberry, peach, grape, and pineapple. You'll find many uses for these motivating stickers.
 Catalog No. 3093-Y $15.95

EASY AS 1-2-3 (1982) *by Constance F. McCarthy and Ann D. Sheehy*
Reproduce these three-step sequences to reinforce language-learning skills. Each of these 20 quick-to-copy sheets shows three clear line illustrations of a child engaged in a specific activity. Your students put the pictures in order so the sequence makes sense. Directions are easy to follow and include specific objectives for coloring, cutting, sequencing, pasting, and oral expression. **Catalog No. 4612-Y $12.95**

Communication Skill Builders

3130 N. Dodge Blvd./P.O. Box 42050
Tucson, Arizona 85733
(602) 323-7500